Research in Stakeholder Theory, 1997-1998: The Sloan Foundation Minigrant Project

Edited by Jeanne M. Logsdon, Donna J. Wood, and Lee E. Benson

THE CLARKSON CENTRE FOR BUSINESS ETHICS
Joseph L. Rotman School of Management
University of Toronto

© Clarkson Centre for Business Ethics 2000
Joseph L. Rotman School of Management
University of Toronto
105 St. George Street
Toronto, ON
Canada M5S 3E6
(416) 978-4930

http://www.mgmt.utoronto.ca/CCBE/
Email: ethics@mgmt.utoronto.ca

Printed in Canada

ISBN 0-7727-8610-0 (paper)

Canadian Cataloguing in Publication Data

Main entry under title:

Research in stakeholder theory, 1997-1998: the Sloan Foundation minigrant project

Includes bibliographical references.

ISBN 0-7727-8610-0

1. Corporations. I. Logsdon, Jeanne M. (Jeanne Marie). II. Wood, Donna J. (Donna J.) III. Benson, Lee E. IV. Alfred P. Sloan Foundation. V. Clarkson Centre for Business Ethics.

HD2731.R47 2000   338.7'4   C99-932083-1

Contents

Part 3: Outcomes and Evaluation

Part 4: Conclusion

Research in Stakeholder Theory, 1997-1998: The Sloan Foundation Minigrant Project

Introduction by Jeanne M. Logsdon,
University of New Mexico, and
Donna J. Wood, University of Pittsburgh

In 1995 Max B.E. Clarkson, University of Toronto, Lee E. Preston, University of Maryland, and Thomas Donaldson, University of Pennsylvania, began the *Redefining the Corporation Project*.[1]

With financial support from the Sloan Foundation, the research program has concentrated on the development of stakeholder theory as a promising way to address many of the questions arising from current efforts to "redefine the corporation" within the economy and society. The co-principal investigators began a "core" research project that involves the study and comparative analysis of large multinational corporations. Part of this work is reflected in the *Principles of Stakeholder Management*[2] which summarizes key features of stakeholder management.

In addition, the group decided to fund, through the Sloan Foundation minigrant program, a number of diverse research projects that would relate to the framework of the overall project. This framework focuses on three dimensions of corporate-stakeholder relations:

1. Context and governance.
2. Management processes.
3. Performance outcomes and evaluation.

We are now pleased to present this volume of reports from the nine minigrant research projects. Five of the nine projects are dissertation-based (Altman, Berman, Davenport, Gerde, and Rowley); the other four represent new projects or continuations of existing research streams. A brief description of the minigrant projects and their fit with the overall program framework appears in Figure 1.

The projects offer a broad spectrum of views on corporate-stakeholder relations based on a variety of research methodologies, including large-scale

Figure 1: Minigrants in the Context of the Redefining the Corporation Project

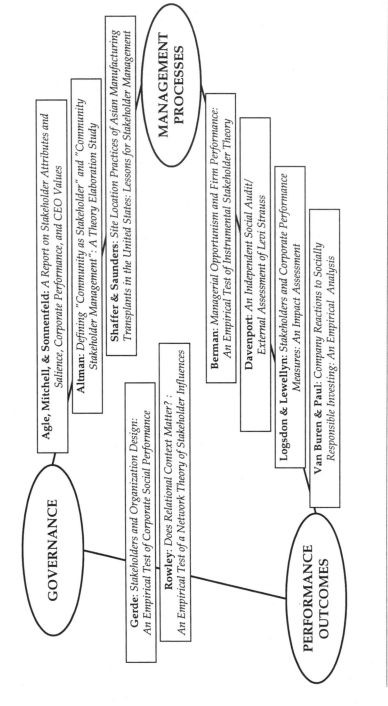

Jeanne M. Logsdon and Donna J. Wood

survey research, case study methods, short-case interviews, quantitative analysis of secondary data, and Delphi methodology. The breadth and quality of these projects, we believe, ensure that they will find scholarly visibility and will spark further research.[3]

This volume concludes with our remarks on social performance measurement, offered at the 1997 Academy of Management meeting (8-13 August, Boston, MA) in an All-Academy Symposium. These remarks, though they focus on measurement and evaluation, point out some of the necessary links that must be drawn among the three project domains—governance, process, and outcomes.

A major purpose of stakeholder theory is to help corporate managers understand their stakeholder environments and manage more effectively within the nexus of relationships that exists for their companies. However, a larger purpose of stakeholder theory is to help corporate managers improve the value of the outcomes of their actions, and minimize the harms to stakeholders. The whole point of stakeholder theory, in fact, lies in what happens when corporations and stakeholders act out their relationships. To this end, we conclude this volume with our view of contributions that stakeholder theory can make to redefine the corporation through a focus on performance measurement.

In May 1998, minigrant recipients attended a two-day conference at the University of Toronto to present preliminary findings from their research. There, they met with the Sloan Foundation program officer, the project's co-principal investigators, members of the project governing board, and selected others. The conference brought minigrant researchers together for the first time, and a coherence and synergy developed among them that will surely have positive impacts far into the future. Since that time, authors have presented their work at professional meetings and submitted their work for publication in academic journals, books, and practitioner outlets.

On behalf of all of the authors, we want to thank the Sloan Foundation and our program officer, Gail Pesyna, for the financial and moral support offered for the research projects. We thank the co-principal investigators, Lee E. Preston, the late Max B.E. Clarkson, and Thomas Donaldson, for their enthusiastic endorsement and support. We thank the other participants in the core project–Sybille Sachs, Edwin Ruhli, and James E. Post–for their participation and feedback. We thank Len Brooks and the staff of the Clarkson Centre for Business Ethics for organizing and superbly providing for the May 1998 conference, and Lee Benson for her editorial work on this volume. We thank Madeleine and Max Clarkson for hosting a wonderful dinner party for conference attendees. To conclude, we offer a special word of thanks to everyone involved in that conference, because it was the last time most of us saw Max Clarkson alive–intense, sparkling, wine glass in hand, intellectually challenging, gracious, and warm.

Jeanne M. Logsdon *jlogsdon@unm.edu*
Robert O. Anderson Schools of Management, University of New Mexico

Donna J. Wood *djwood@katz.pitt.edu*
Joseph M. Katz Graduate School of Business, University of Pittsburgh

---

[1] The *Project* website is maintained by The Clarkson Centre for Business Ethics and can be accessed at: *http://www.mgmt.utoronto.ca/~stake/*

[2] Clarkson Centre for Business Ethics. 1999. *Principles of Stakeholder Management.* Toronto: CCBE.

[3] In many cases, the project reports were shortened to fit into this volume. Readers interested in further detail are encouraged to contact individual authors directly.

Part 1

Governance

Stakeholders and Organization Design: An Empirical Test of Corporate Social Performance

Virginia W. Gerde, University of New Mexico

Introduction

Corporations that do not respond to stakeholder pressures and social expectations risk losing legitimacy (DiMaggio and Powell, 1983). To address growing societal expectations of social performance, some corporations have adopted design features believed to be "ethical," and consulting firms have promoted the use of "ethical design features." However, the normative underpinnings of these design features and their effectiveness for corporate social performance (CSP) have been under-addressed.

Although Freeman's (1984) stakeholder theory constitutes a major theoretical advance in incorporating ethical considerations into the construction of organization design, little has been done to develop specific, normatively based design principles for corporations. Scholars have continued to call for normative underpinnings for stakeholder theory (Freeman, 1994; Donaldson and Preston, 1995; Phillips, 1997); nonetheless, no specific design principles or organizational design features have been developed. Stephens (1991) developed the Rawlsian model of the organization, and Stephens, *et al.* (1997) suggested design features appropriate to meet the design principles of a just organization. The present study furthers this research by empirically testing these design principles.

The predominant definitions of for-profit organizational goals and performance are economic in nature—efficiency, economic growth, and economic survival (Lewin and Minton, 1986). Organization theorists (e.g., Daft, 1992) recognize that the purpose of organization design is to carry out the organization's goals. Thus, organization design must be congruent with goals if the organization is to perform effectively. Current theories of organization design take into account the economic performance goals, but they fail to address the extra-economic goals of CSP. Therefore, existing prescriptive design principles (e.g., Lawrence and Lorsch, 1967; Duncan, 1972), while useful for the attainment of economic goals, do not identify how to attain

CSP goals.

The purpose of this study is to describe and test an ideal-type model of organization design to achieve the goal of justice. The model of a just organization (Stephens, 1991) is based on Rawls' (1971) theory of justice and Max Weber's (1978) social action category of *wertrational* (or value-rationality) and is presented in Stephens (1991) and Stephens, *et al.* (1997). To test the model, corporations are surveyed for the presence of specific design features to determine whether corporations with design features similar to those of the ideal type of just organization have better social performance, as measured by higher CSP ratings, than those corporations whose designs deviate from the ideal type.

A Normative Basis for Stakeholder Theory

Although any value or principle–aesthetic, epistemological, hedonistic, or ethical–may be selected as terminal by an individual or a group and thus be used in the design of a value-rational organization, Stephens and colleagues (Stephens, 1991; Stephens, *et al.*, 1997) chose the ethical value of justice (e.g., Kant, 1938; Hume, 1965; Rawls, 1971) as the terminal value around which to construct organization design. Justice, as an organizing principle, has been described as the value that best captures organizations' efforts to meet the needs of a wide variety of internal and external stakeholders (Keeley, 1978, 1988; Freeman, 1984; Donaldson and Preston, 1995). By addressing the distribution of costs and benefits, justice also addresses the main concerns of corporate social responsibility (CSR). The concept of justice aids in the consideration of (a) what stakeholders would want from an organization and (b) how an organization may distribute cost and benefits among stakeholders.

An *a priori* or general model of normative organizing principles is deduced from Rawls' *Theory of Justice* (1971) by Stephens (1991). The design model consists of five principles, described below. Holding to the impartiality axiom, the just organization design necessarily extends to all constituencies or stakeholders, not merely to employees or to shareholders. Secondly, the interests of the stakeholder group most likely to be negatively affected must be given the most weight in a particular decision. Relatively low benefit dispersion is similar to the differential respect of interests in that the inequities in the distribution of costs and benefits must be to the benefit of those least-advantaged. For example, pay scales need not be equal throughout the organization, but if there is a difference in pay, it must be justifiable on the grounds that the difference will generate benefits for the organization that will be shared with all workers. Finally, providing opportunities for voice and moral agency in the organization by all the organization's members is critical.

Virginia W. Gerde

Research Question

I hypothesized that the more an organization emulates the ideal type of just organization, the better its social performance will be as measured by higher CSP ratings. *Do just organizations (organizations that are designed around the value of justice for their stakeholders) have better CSP ratings than those organizations that do not have the design features of just organizations?*

Methodology

Corporations were surveyed to determine the extent to which they embodied these design characteristics, and the deviation of each responding corporation from the ideal-type profile was calculated (Alexander and Randolph, 1985; Drazin and Van de Ven, 1985). This deviation distance was then compared to the social performance measurement to empirically test the design-performance relationship.

In the systems approach, an ideal-type profile is compared to the profile of a sample organization (Drazin and Van de Ven, 1985; Van de Ven and Drazin, 1985; Gresov, Drazin and Van de Ven, 1989). Deviations of the sample organization from the ideal-type profile are determined by measuring the "distance" of each organization from its location in multidimensional space to the location of the ideal-type profile in the same multidimensional space. This "distance" is known as the Euclidean distance or a summary distance metric.

The presence of the design features is determined by a survey of the firms included in the Kinder, Lydenberg, and Domini (KLD) social performance database. These features are used to rate each firm along the five design dimensions, and each firm is "plotted" in multidimensional space, from which the Euclidean distance from the sample firm to the ideal-type firm may be calculated. Each firm's design dimensions received an ordinal rating from 1 to 5 based on the presence of design features identified in the survey responses. With a distance from the ideal-type profile to the firm calculated for each sample firm, these relative distances may then be correlated to the CSP rating.

Survey Techniques

In the KLD database, approximately 650 corporations are rated on various social issues or CSP dimensions, which are used in this study to determine the dependent variable. The KLD database provides a snapshot analysis of the context-design-performance relationship of some of the world's largest publicly traded corporations. Surveys were mailed to a member of top management, such as the General Counsel or a Vice President, for all corporations in the KLD database.

Variables

Van de Ven and Ferry (1980) provide a framework for analyzing the effectiveness of organization design at the macro-organizational level: context, design, and outcome. The context is determined by two variables: size and industry. Adapting the design dimensions of Lewin and Stephens (1993) and the design elements identified by Stephens (1993), the following design dimensions were used to determine the independent variable (Euclidean distance from the ideal-type profile): structural configuration, human resources policies and incentives, control systems, strategic planning, and organizational ethos. The outcome dimension is measured by CSP, following Van de Ven and Ferry's (1980) suggestion of assessing the outcome of an organization not solely in economic terms, but also in terms of its impact on society. The macro-organizational dimensions for this study, and their associated design features and/or measurement, are listed in Table 1.

The dependent variable is the overall CSP rating from the KLD database which is based on the equally weighted sum total of the CSP scores on various KLD sub-dimensions. The KLD database has several general sub-dimensions on which it rates each firm: Community, Employee Relations, Environment, Product, Diversity, Non-U.S. Operations, and Other.

Results

Descriptive statistics for the context dimensions, or control variables, follow a brief description of the survey results. After the design dimensions are individually analyzed, the use of these dimensions to determine a deviation distance is presented. As described earlier, the deviation distance is the Euclidean distance for each firm from the ideal-type profile. The distance is then tested with the outcome dimension, or performance measure, to determine any correlation with design and performance.

A total of 120 usable surveys were returned by June 14, 1998, for an 18.3 percent return rate. The majority of surveys were returned within the first six weeks, with an average return time of twenty-seven days. A concern in studies such as this is social desirability response (SDR) in the responding sample; however, the responding sample was not significantly different than the total population (all 655 firms in the KLD database) for the control variables or the dependent variable (CSP score). That is, firms scoring below average were just as likely to send back a response as firms that scored above average.

Control Variables

Firm size was taken as the number of employees reported to Standard and Poor's (1998). If this number was not available in this source, size was taken from the KLD database. For the responding sample, the average number of employees is 30,360, with the smallest firm reporting 148 employees and the

Table 1: Macro-Organizational Dimensions and Associated Design Features or Measurement

Macro-Organizational Dimensions	Variables	Design Features or Measurement
Context (Control Variables)	Organization Size	Number of employees
	Organizational Domain	Industry category
Design (Independent Variables)	Structural Configuration	Configuration of board of directors
		Scanning position
		Ethics or social responsibility officer
		Ethics or social responsibility department
		Management committee for ethics
	Human Resources Policies and Incentives	Ethics hotline
		Open-door policy
		Ethics training programs
		Employee participation on ethics committee and/or strategic planning
	Control Systems	Ethics audit
		Compensation, evaluation, and incentive (CEI) plan
	Strategic Planning	Strategic planning (inclusion of stakeholders)
	Organizational Ethos	Corporate credo or code of ethics
		Promulgation of corporate credo or code of ethics
Outcome (Dependent Variable)	Corporate Social Performance	CSP measures

largest reporting 371,702 employees. The largest subgroup ranged from 10,001 to 50,000 employees. The responding sample was very similar in distribution to the KLD population, with the greatest difference (3 percent) in the number of firms in the 5,001 to 10,000 employees size.

Each firm was placed in one of ten industry categories used in the KLD database. The distribution of industries in the responding sample was similar to the distribution of industries in the database overall. The one exception is that of the natural resources category (e.g., chemicals, forest and paper products, mining, natural gas, and oil), which accounts for 14.4 percent of the entire database but 20.8 percent of the returned surveys.

Independent Variables
In this section, the results for each dimension are reported, and the subsequent ratings of firms for each dimension are presented.

Structural Configuration Design Dimension
The activity of corporate social scanning, or scanning the environment for social trends and issues that may impact the firm, was undertaken at either the board or the management level. Approximately one-third of the firms (31 percent) had a committee or member of the board responsible for scanning the corporate environment for social trends or social issues, and 47 percent had such a position or department at the management level.

The structure of the board of directors was examined by looking at the presence of committees for stakeholder issues, the appointment of a board member to address these issues, and the presence of a board-level corporate social environment scanning position.

Firms were more likely to have a board committee or appointed board member to represent the concerns of stakeholders (e.g., Corporate Responsibility Committee and Community Affairs) than to have an outside member of the board from a specific stakeholder group. Product and supplier issues received the lowest representation on boards or by committees (in 23 percent and 15 percent of firms, respectively); however, several respondents wrote that these issues were considered implicitly by their board. Almost half of the firms, 43 percent, responded that they had an employee representative on the board, although several respondents said the representative was a human resources officer, which is more a management representation of employees. The environment-as-a-stakeholder received considerable attention, as 38 percent of the respondents indicated the board had a committee or representative designated for environmental issues. The greatest percentage of representation of stakeholders was that of the public interest: 50 percent of the respondents claimed representation of the public interest, sometimes through a board committee for social responsibility. Approximately one-third of the firms indicated that there was a committee or board member responsible for community issues (34 percent), minority issues (37.5 percent), or women's issues (32.5 percent).

While the presence of committees on a board of directors is indicative of the concerns of the firm, the emphasis seems to be on the protection of the firm from these stakeholders. Based on the comments on the returned surveys, I believe many boards had designated representatives or committees (formal or informal) to consider various stakeholders, but only to the extent that the stakeholders could impact the organization, not to examine the impact of the firm on the stakeholders.

The representation of stakeholders by outside members on the boards of directors was significantly less than that by inside members or committees. Approximately 36 percent of the firms have an outside member of the board from the community, specifically as a representative of the community. Based on the annual reports of many of these firms, the outside member is usually a businessperson from the surrounding community, whose interests may be solely economic and not representative of the community-as-stakeholder interests, regardless of how community is defined. For example, on the board of a natural resources firm, the community member is the president of a local bank. Other stakeholder groups were rarely represented. Public interest groups, trade associations, and consumers are represented by outside board members at 7.5 percent, 6.7 percent, and 5.8 percent, respectively. Employees and the natural environment were represented in 4 percent and 5 percent of the firms, respectively, while diversity issues or non-profit groups for minorities and women were represented in about 4 percent of the responding firms. Note that few firms had members from stakeholder groups other than investors on the board of directors. The largest percentage of representation was for the community, with 35.8 percent of the firms having a community member on the board of directors.

The design of management structure to address ethical issues, issues of social responsibility, and stakeholder concerns varied among the firms. Approximately two-thirds of the respondents (67.5 percent) indicated that they had a department or functional area specifically responsible for promoting ethics or social responsibility within the firm. In general, based on the comments from respondents, these departments or functional areas were not exclusively for promoting ethics or social responsibility, but rather had such a task as part of other responsibilities such as internal audit, legal affairs, or public affairs.

Approximately 70 percent of the firms also responded that they had a member of top management specifically responsible for ethics or social responsibility. When asked for specifics about the titles of this person, and the person to whom s/he reported, a range of answers was received. Two firms had full-time ethics officers who reported to the CEO and the Board of Directors. Other firms had executives who held the title of Ethics Officer in addition to other titles such as General Counsel or a Senior Vice President. For other firms, the responsibility was part of a vice president's job, even without the additional title, and several firms had two members of top management. Approximately one-tenth of the respondents (9 percent) listed the CEO as the responsible executive, reporting to the Chairman of the Board of Directors. The reporting relationships also varied. The sample was evenly split between reporting to the CEO and to the Board. One firm even had the Vice President of Internal Audit as the member of top management who reported to the Board of Directors.

Overall, two-thirds of the firms had a department or specific area for ethics and/or social responsibility (67.5 percent), a member of top management specifically responsible for ethics or social responsibility (69 percent), and 56 percent had both design features. Surprisingly, 23 percent of the firms had neither a department nor an officer specifically responsible for ethics and/or social responsibility.

Another design element that was found either in conjunction with a specific department or person responsible for ethics or social responsibility is that of the management committee for such issues. Of the respondents, 42.5 percent indicated that they had a management committee for ethics and/or social responsibility. Further inquiry on the composition of this committee showed that 12.5 percent had non-management employees on the committee, and only 5 percent had people from outside the firm on the committee. Only three firms reported the inclusion of both non-management employees and outside members on the ethics committee.

Human Resources Policies and Incentives (HRPI) Design Dimension
The majority of firms had at least one of the design elements present. A formal "open door" policy for employees to speak with managers was reported by two-thirds of the firms (67 percent). Almost the same number (65 percent) have an ethics hotline within the firm for employees to ask questions or to report possible ethics violations. Approximately one-third, or 37 percent, of the firms included employees in the strategic planning process through focus groups or consultation and representation in the process. Of the 43 percent of firms that have a management committee for ethics or social responsibility, about one-third (35 percent) include employees on the committee (for a total of 15 percent of all the firms). Only 4 percent of the firms had an outside member of the board and an employee group representative.

Control Systems Design Dimension
Of the respondents, 60.8 percent (73 firms) reported that they regularly conduct an ethics or a social audit. A higher percentage, 77.5 percent (93 firms), reported having compensation, evaluation, and incentive (CEI) plans for managers based upon extra-economic goals as well as economic goals. Ap-

Virginia W. Gerde

proximately 45 percent of the firms have both design elements present, 46.7 percent have either an audit or a CEI plan, and 8.3 percent have neither.

Strategic Planning Design Dimension
Respondents were asked how six constituencies (stakeholder groups) were included in the strategic planning process. The most-represented group in the strategic planning process was the Customer group, at 40 percent. Employees and the Environment were both included in strategic planning in 36.7 percent of the firms. Suppliers and the Community were involved in the strategic planning process in 29.2 percent and 21.7 percent of the firms, respectively. Of all the constituencies, Government was integrated into strategic planning process the least: it was included by only 15.8 percent of firms, most of which were in the utilities industry, primarily to deal with the impact of current or pending regulations.

While the natural environment is a difficult stakeholder to include in the strategic planning process as another voice or vote, the environment was explicitly taken into account in 36.7 percent of firms, primarily those in the natural resources and drugs/medical services industries. These industries may exhibit more regulation and public scrutiny than other industries.

Organizational Ethos Design Dimension
Corporate mission statements, vision statements, or codes of ethics were analyzed to determine the degree of inclusion of stakeholders and the attitudes towards them. Only five firms addressed the avoidance of harm to at least two stakeholders by the organization. Many firms, particularly those in the natural resources and utilities industries, had adopted a set of principles to protect the environment and to minimize the impact of the organization on the natural environment, and these firms were rated a "4." The other industry category highly represented in the ratings of "4" and "5" was the drugs and medical services category, which expounded a concern for the protection of the consumer and society from harm by the organization's products.

Dependent Variable
When compared to the entire KLD database, the group of respondents had approximately the same CSP scores. The mean score for all the firms in the KLD database is 21.580 (standard deviation = 3.185); that of the responding sample is 21.617 (standard deviation = 2.467), and an ANOVA one-way comparison indicated no significant difference between the two scores.

Deviation Distance
A deviation distance was calculated for each firm as the Euclidean distance from the ideal-type profile along five dimensions, referred to as DISTANCE in this section. These distances were then compared to each firm's CSP score.

Deviation distance did not correlate with the total CSP score, as shown in Table 2. Size accounted for most of the variability in the adjusted R^2, as the coefficient for size was significant (.002), but the coefficient for DISTANCE was not significant (.200). This indicates that deviation distance is not correlated with performance for all firms (all industry categories) as a whole. Subsequent analyses were done by industry category to control for the effects of industry category.

Table 2: Regression Analysis

$CSP = \beta_0 + \beta_1$ SIZE $+ \beta_2$ DISTANCE	$R^2 = 0.063$, F = 4.920 (0.009)
	$\beta_1 = -0.296$, significant at 0.00
	$\beta_2 = -0.122$, significant at 0.200
$CSP2 = \beta_0 + \beta_1$ SIZE $+ \beta_2$ DISTANCE2	$R^2 = 0.103$, F = 7.675 (0.001)
	$\beta_1 = -0.329$, significant at 0.00
	$\beta_2 = 0.036$, significant at 0.7051

Correlation and regression analyses were conducted within each industry category for DISTANCE and CSP. The correlation results indicated no association at the .05 significance level or better. The regression analyses indicated that size accounted for some variation in the CSP score, but the coefficients for the DISTANCE variable were not significant.

A modification to the calculation of DISTANCE was made to examine the influence of the organizational-ethos design dimension. A new deviation distance was calculated using the four design dimensions of structural configuration, HRPI, control systems, and strategic planning. This new deviation distance, based on the design dimensions, is termed DISTANCE2. A different calculation of the CSP score with only five of the KLD sub-dimensions indicates more association with the distance measure. This second CSP score is based on the equal-weighting aggregate of the Community, the Employees, the Environment, the Product, and the Other sub-dimensions and is termed CSP2. The regression analysis, shown in Table 2, shows no significant relationship between the modified distance measurement and the CSP score. Taking industry into account, there was no correlation between deviation distance and CSP, except in the transportation industry (which had only four firms in the responding sample). Regression analyses performed by industry showed no significant relationship between organization design and the social performance measurement.

Discussion and Conclusions

I hypothesized that corporations designed around the value of justice have better CSP ratings than corporations lacking the design features of a just organization. However, the results do not support this hypothesis. Deviation distance (distance from the ideal-type profile) did not correlate with CSP, nor did regression analysis show a relationship between CSP and deviation distance. Firms with more design features of the just organization did not have significantly higher CSP scores. A regression analysis of size and deviation distance accounts for only a portion (6.3 percent) of the variation. Of that variation, firm size was the most influential variable, and its coefficient was significant ($p < .01$), but the coefficient for deviation distance was not significant.

Why were firms having more of the design features of a just organization not rated higher as a group than firms having fewer of the design features? There are several possible explanations that center around two main problems. The first problematic area is the measurement of CSP. This area is relatively recent (about thirty years) and there are no widely accepted ways to measure CSP, as there are widely accepted accounting practices and financial measurements of economic performance.

A second possibility is that the design features themselves are in place because of external expectations, or through institutional mimetic isomorphism (DiMaggio and Powell, 1983), and are not necessarily effective. If they are not effective, the presence or absence of these features would not affect performance. These design features may be incorporated because (1) the features are rationalized *myths*, generally believed to be effective and are now institutionalized as rules and patterns (Meyer and Rowan, 1977); or (2) other firms, especially those that are economically successful or socially prestigious, adopt them (Powell and DiMaggio, 1991).

A third explanation may be related to the setting of standards for establishing performance criteria. If cause-effect relations and standards of performance are unclear (as they are for social performance), social tests are used to determine effectiveness (Thompson, 1967). Upheld by consensus or authority, social tests gain legitimacy by who sanctions them; therefore, in an institutionalized environment, these organizations rely on these social tests to validate their effectiveness or performance. The CSP measures studied here are a social test, with corporations and investors relying "on external criteria of worth" (Meyer and Rowan, 1977: 350).

Scholars have studied particular design features that are presumed to promote ethical outcomes for organizations; however, these design features have not been examined for, or derived from, normative justifications. The general model of a just organization (Stephens, 1991) provides normative organization design principles based on Rawls' theory of justice (1971) and consistent with Freeman's (1984) stakeholder framework and Weber's *wertrational* social action category (1978). This study is the first to test this model of how normatively based design principles may relate to the outcome of CSP. Although this study showed no direct association between the presence of design features identified for a just organization and CSP, it is a first step in the refining and testing of normative organization design principles called for by Freeman (1994). Future research should illuminate the relationship between organizational design and CSP, including design dimensions for social performance, CSP measurement, and design features for a just organization.

Virginia Gerde (*gerde@anderson.unm.edu*) is Assistant Professor in Organizational Studies at the Robert O. Anderson Schools of Management, University of New Mexico, Albuquerque, NM 87131-1221. This report is based on her dissertation research.

References

Alexander, J.W., and Randolph, A.W. 1985. The fit between technology and structure as a predictor of performance in nursing subunits. *Academy of Management Journal*, 28 (4): 844-859.

Daft, R.L. 1992. *Organization theory and design*. 4th ed. St. Paul, MN: West Publishing.

DiMaggio, P., and Powell, W. 1983. The iron cage revisited: Institutional isomorphism and collective rationality in organizational fields. *American Sociological Review*, 48 (April): 147-160.

Donaldson, T., and Preston, L.E. 1995. The stakeholder theory of the corporation: Concepts, evidence, and implications. *Academy of Management Review*, 20 (1): 65-91.

Drazin, R., and Van de Ven, A.H. 1985. Alternative forms of fit in contingency theory. *Administrative Science Quarterly*, 30 (4) (Dec.): 514-539.

Duncan, R.B. 1972. Characteristics of organizational environments and perceived environmental uncertainty. *Administrative Science Quarterly*, 17 (3) (Sept.): 313-327.

Freeman, R.E. 1984. *Strategic management: A stakeholder approach*. Boston, MA: Pitman.

Freeman, R.E. 1994. The politics of stakeholder theory: Some future directions. *Business Ethics Quarterly*, 4 (4): 409-421.

Gresov, C., Drazin, R., and Van de Ven, A.H. 1989. Work-unit task uncertainty, design, and morale. *Organization Studies*, 10 (1): 45-62.

Hume, D. 1978. *A treatise of human nature*. Ed. L.A. Bigge; text revisions and variant readings by P.H. Nidditch. 2nd ed. New York: Oxford University Press. [Originally published 1777.]

Kant, I. 1938. *The fundamental principles of the metaphysics of ethics*. Trans. O. Manthey-Zorn. New York: Appleton Century Crofts. [Originally published 1855.]

Keeley, M. 1978. A social-justice approach to organizational evaluation. *Administrative Science Quarterly*, 23 (2) (June): 272-292.

Keeley, M. 1988. *A social-contract theory of organizations*. Notre Dame, IN: University of Notre Dame Press.

Lawrence, P.R., and Lorsch, J.W. 1967. *Organization and environment: Managing differentiation and integration*. Boston: Division of Research, Graduate School of Business Administration, Harvard University.

Lewin, A.Y., and Minton, J. 1986. Determining organizational effectiveness: Another look, and a research agenda. *Management Science*, 32 (5) (May): 514-538.

Lewin, A.Y., and Stephens, C.U. 1993. Designing postindustrial organizations: Combining theory and practice. In: *Organizational change and redesign: Ideas and insights for improving performance*, ed. George P. Huber and William H. Glick: 393-409. New York: Oxford University Press.

Meyer, J.W., and Rowan, B. 1977. Institutional organizations: Formal structure as myth and ceremony. *American Journal of Sociology*, 83 (2): 340-363.

Phillips, R.A. 1997. A principle of fairness. *Business Ethics Quarterly*, 7 (1): 51-66.

Powell, W.W., and DiMaggio, P.J., eds. 1991. *The new institutionalism in organizational analysis*. Chicago: University of Chicago Press.

Rawls, J. 1971. *A theory of justice*. Cambridge, MA: Belknap Press of Harvard University Press.

Standard and Poor's Corp. 1998. *Register of corporations, directors, and executives, United States and Canada*. 1998. New York: The Corporation.

Stephens, C.U. 1991. *The design dimensions of the just organization: A neo-Weberian ideal type*. Doctoral dissertation, Duke University, Durham, NC. [Theoretical development.]

Stephens, C.U. 1993. *The design dimensions of the just organization: A neo-Weberian ideal type*. Doctoral dissertation, Duke University, Durham, NC. [Qualitative study.]

Stephens, C.U., Gerde, V.W., Wokutch, R.E., and Watson, G. 1997. The value-rational organization: A Rawlsian perspective on structure. In *Proceedings of the Eighth Annual Meeting of the International Association for Business and Society held in Destin, FL, 6-9 March 1997*, ed. J. Weber and K. Rehbein: 119-124.

Thompson, J.D. 1967. *Organizations in action*. New York: McGraw-Hill.

Van de Ven, A.H., and Drazin, R. 1985. The concept of fit in contingency theory. *Research in Organizational Behavior*, 7: 333-365.

Van de Ven, A.H., and Ferry, D.L. 1980. *Measuring and assessing organizations*. New York: Wiley.

Weber, M. 1978. *Economy and society: An outline of interpretive sociology*. Ed. G. Roth and C. Wittich; trans. Ephraim Fischoff, *et al*. Berkeley: University of California Press. [Translation of *Wirtschaft und Gesellschaft. Grundriss der verstehenden Soziologie*, based on the 4th German ed. Originally published 1910.]

Does Relational Context Matter?: An Empirical Test of a Network Theory of Stakeholder Influences

Timothy J. Rowley, University of Toronto

Introduction

Freeman (1984) suggests that one of the reasons the stakeholder perspective holds promise for management scholars and practitioners is that it provides a means for dealing with multiple stakeholders and multiple conflicting interests. While focusing on individual stakeholder relationships is appropriate for exploring the stakeholders' interests and behaviors, it cannot be extended to predict how focal organizations respond to their stakeholders, because each firm faces a different set of stakeholders aggregated into unique patterns of influence. A firm does not simply respond to each stakeholder individually, but rather to the interaction of multiple influences from its entire stakeholder set. Therefore, according to those believing that a "system-centered" theory will be more valuable than the firm-centered perspective in understanding stakeholder relations, it is necessary to explain how the multiple, interdependent relationships in an organization's network interact. Then, stakeholder influences can be more precisely predicted and organizations' responsibilities more easily prescribed (Rowley, 1997; Wood, 1994).

Although the relational context has received more attention from stakeholder researchers in recent years, there has been no empirical work offered to support propositions suggesting that a given organization-stakeholder relationship is influenced by the surrounding mesh of relationships. It is still only a matter of theoretical conjecture that the relational context is meaningful to stakeholder relationships. In this paper, I empirically test whether relational context impacts how organizations treat their stakeholders. The study is designed to empirically test Rowley's (1997) theoretical argument that the structure of a stakeholder relationship network influences how organizations treat their multiple and interdependent stakeholders.

Background

Social Network Analysis and Stakeholder Influences

The social network analysis literature provides tools for developing and testing theories pertaining to the relational context of stakeholder relationships. The aim of network analysis is "to reveal the structural form beneath the apparent content of social relations" (Kilduff and Krackhardt, 1994: 105). The stakeholder framework and social network analysis are similar since both perspectives focus on ties between a series of social actors. Social network analysis offers stakeholder researchers a means for stretching the analytical focus beyond dyadic organization-stakeholder ties, which are commonly the focus of stakeholder research.

The theoretical framework within which I analyze the effect of the relational context on how organizations treat their stakeholders involves Rowley's (1997) structural theory of stakeholder influences. From this perspective, the density of the network and the focal organization's centrality in the network–two structural factors of stakeholder networks–are argued to be influential in determining how organizations interact with their stakeholders.

Density measures the degree of interconnectedness between an organization's stakeholders. Oliver (1991) suggests that densely connected networks allow for information exchanges and the coordination of activities. By virtue of having many ties between them, stakeholders can efficiently communicate with one another. Moreover, Meyer and Rowan (1977) argue that institutional norms are diffused through relational (stakeholder) networks. As these linkages become more dense, norms and behaviors become more similar, which tends to produce collectivism and coordination in the network (Galaskiewicz and Wasserman, 1989; Oliver, 1991). Thus, the product of a highly dense network of stakeholders is the creation of an efficient communication mechanism and shared behavioral expectations across the network. Under these conditions, stakeholders can more easily build coalitions (Mintzberg, 1983), and collectively monitor and pressure the focal organization. As a result, other things being equal, the focal organization will conform to its well-organized stakeholders' expectations (Rowley, 1997). In contrast, a less dense network does not afford stakeholders efficient communication nor create shared behavior expectations; therefore, stakeholders will not be able to collectively monitor or sanction (positively or negatively) the focal organization. Thus, organizations surrounded by a densely connected set of stakeholders will face stronger pressures and will need to conform to stakeholder expectations more than organizations operating in less densely connected stakeholder networks. The hypothesis (H) can be stated as:

H1: As the density of the stakeholder network increases, the focal

Timothy J. Rowley

organization's resistance to stakeholder pressures decreases.

Betweenness centrality, one of several centrality measures, represents a social actor's structural prominence or power (Brass and Burkhardt, 1993; Freeman, 1979). Centrality is the degree to which an actor in a network falls on a path between other actors (stakeholders) in the network. Thus, if actor A can only reach actor B via actor C, then actor C is highly central in the network and possesses power over any exchanges between actors A and B. Rowley (1997) argues that if the focal organization occupies a highly central position, it can control exchanges between its stakeholders. As a central player in the network, the focal organization is in a gatekeeper position which it can use to influence the formation of shared behavioral expectations and manipulate information exchanges (Freeman, 1979; Scott, 1991). In this powerful position, the focal organization can afford to be less cooperative with its fragmented stakeholders. In other words, it will resist its stakeholders' pressures to meet their expectations:

H2: As the focal organization's centrality increases, its resistance to stakeholder pressures increases.

Network Configurations
By considering the interaction of network density and focal organization centrality, Rowley (1997) provides further predictions regarding how focal organizations will respond to stakeholders under the simultaneous influences of these structural factors. He argues that the interaction of high and low degrees of network density and high and low degrees of the focal organization's centrality will lead to four types of organizational responses to stakeholders (Figure 1). Density and centrality are both continuous variables, however, and categorically placing firms into distinct classifications, such as "high" or "low," is problematic. Moreover, depending on a firm's centrality and the density surrounding it, the firm may exhibit components of more than one type of behavior. For example, a firm occupying a centrality position characterized as "medium" in relative terms and existing in a "medium" density network will likely portray elements of all four response behaviors. However, as density and centrality move away from these medium levels toward more extreme positions–either increasing or decreasing–one of the four focal firm response behaviors will emerge as the dominant behavior. The logic supporting Rowley's (1997) four behaviors and the hypotheses in this study is briefly summarized below.

Compromiser
When a focal firm occupies a central position in a densely connected network, it faces a well-organized group of stakeholders capable of collectively influencing the focal organization. However, the focal organization is also

Figure 1: Structural Influences and Firm Behaviors

		Centrality of the Focal Organization	
		High	Low
Density of the Stakeholder Network	High	COMPROMISER	SUBORDINATE
	Low	COMMANDER	SOLITARIAN

(Source: Rowley, 1997: 901.)

in a powerful position and is capable of influencing exchanges within the stakeholder network. Both institutional and resource dependence theorists argue that an organization will attempt to negotiate with its inter-organizational partners (stakeholders) in this situation in order to reduce environmental uncertainty (Oliver, 1991; Pfeffer and Salancik, 1978). As the density of the network and focal organization centrality both increase, the focal organization will attempt to negotiate, balance and pacify its stakeholders in order to reach a mutually acceptable solution. Rowley (1997) uses the term *compromiser* to represent this negotiating behavioral type. Thus:

H3a: *The density of relationships among stakeholders is positively related to the focal organization's compromiser behavior.*

H3b: *The focal organization's centrality is positively related to the focal organization's compromiser behavior.*

Subordinate
Under a high density/low centrality condition, the focal organization is in a vulnerable, peripheral position, unable to influence its stakeholders, who are capable of collectively monitoring and sanctioning the focal organization (Rowley, 1997). Under these conditions, the focal organization is at the mercy of its well-organized stakeholders and will adopt a *subordinate* role in which it complies with its stakeholders' expectations. Thus:

H4a: *The density of relationships among stakeholders is positively related to the focal organization's subordinate behavior.*

H4b: *The focal organization's centrality is negatively related to the focal organization's subordinate behavior.*

Commander
In a low density/high centrality structure, the focal firm is well positioned in a sparsely connected network. The focal organization holds a powerful structural advantage over its stakeholders, who will not be able to collectively exert pressure on the organization due to their sparsely connected network (Jacobs, 1974; Mintzberg, 1983). Under these conditions, the focal organization has the power to significantly influence exchanges throughout the network. As density decreases and focal organization centrality increases, the focal organization will increasingly adopt a *commander* role, attempting to control and dominate its stakeholder relationships. Thus:

H5a: The density of relationships among stakeholders is negatively related to the focal organization's commander behavior.

H5b: The focal organization's centrality is positively related to the focal organization's commander behavior.

Solitarian
Finally, when the focal firm is in a low centrality position within a sparsely connected stakeholder network, it will be unable to influence its stakeholders, but it will also face few constraints from its fragmented stakeholders (Oliver, 1991). The focal organization will be somewhat isolated from its stakeholders and will be able to conceal and buffer its activities (Powell, 1988). Thus, focal organizations occupying a low centrality position in a sparsely connected stakeholder network will attempt to avoid stakeholder pressures by obscuring and buffering their activities. Rowley (1997) labels firms adopting this secretive behavioral type as *solitarians*. Thus:

H6a: The density of relationships among stakeholders is negatively related to the focal organization's solitarian behavior.

H6b: The focal organization's centrality is negatively related to the focal organization's solitarian behavior.

In addition to testing whether density and centrality influence how firms behave, I argue that density and centrality also affect firm performance. Freeman (1984: 52) argues that stakeholders can affect, or are affected by, the achievement of an organization's mission, and "if business organizations are to be successful in the current and future environment then executives must take multiple stakeholders into account." Ansoff (1965) argues that the degree to which stakeholders can impact organizational performance depends on several situational variables.

A firm's centrality and the density of its network play a role in determining the impact stakeholders have on a firm's performance. Stakeholders in a dense network can efficiently communicate with other stakeholders and have the ability to collectively monitor and punish the focal organization. In this environment, stakeholders are capable of influencing a firm's performance. Firms surrounded by a well-connected set of stakeholders will not be able to focus all of their resources on purely economic, self-interested goals because they will need to cooperate with their powerful stakeholders and allocate resources toward their interests. As a result, such a firm's financial performance will be lower than if it were not forced to consider its stakeholders. In a low-density environment, however, stakeholders do not have access to an efficient communication system, and lack the collective monitoring and punishing capabilities available in a dense network. Thus, in a sparsely connected network, and assuming firms are driven by economic self-interest (Williamson, 1970), the focal firm can, and will, focus more of its resources and strategy on the corporation's own economic goals. As a result, the firm's financial performance will be higher in a low-density network than in a high-density network. This discussion leads to the following hypothesis:

H7: Density is negatively related to firm performance.

In addition, firm centrality is associated with firm performance. A firm occupying a highly central position is capable of controlling exchanges across the network and influencing the behavioral expectations established among the network's actors. In this gatekeeper role, the focal firm faces less pressure to conform to stakeholder expectations than firms in low centrality positions. While occupying this powerful position, a central firm can predominantly focus its resources on economic objectives. Firms occupying low centrality positions, however, are not capable of influencing exchanges among actors in the network. These organizations must be more attentive to stakeholder interests and will need to allocate resources toward their stakeholders' objectives. Thus:

H8: Centrality is positively related to firm performance.

Methods

Selection of Networks

To control many of the environmental and industry-level factors, the two networks used in this study focused on specific industries: one network was constructed for the steel-producing industry and another for the semiconductor manufacturing industry. The selection of these industries was dictated by two decision criteria. First, as discussed below, the network data were collected primarily from published reports, and, therefore, required well-documented relationships between firms. Both the steel producer and semiconductor manufacturer industries were followed closely by major newspa-

Timothy J. Rowley

pers, and business and trade publications. Second, the network boundaries-who is and who is not in the network (Gulati, 1995; Oliver, 1988)-needed to be reasonably clear. Because both industries in this study were capital- and knowledge- intensive, firms tended to be large players focusing exclusively on, or dedicating distinct business units to, steel or semiconductor manufacturing. The existence of large firms and the lack of peripheral players provided a reasonably clear picture of the firms within each industry (Gulati, 1995).

Type of Linkage

Researchers empirically examining networks at the organizational level have predominately relied on strategic alliance (Gulati, 1995; Hagedoorn, 1993; Hagedoorn and Schakenraad, 1994; Madhavan, 1996), or interlocking directorate relationships (Allen, 1982; Burt, 1983; Laumann and Pappi, 1976; Levine, 1972; Mintz and Schwartz, 1981; Mintz and Schwartz, 1985) for constructing industry networks. Strategic alliances were chosen as the focus of this study: these include joint ventures, non-equity cooperative agreements, such as joint research and development programs, joint marketing and manufacturing initiatives, licensing agreements and long-term supplier arrangements (Contractor and Lorange, 1988).

As conduits for organizational learning and knowledge transfer, strategic alliances are instrumental in affecting how firms behave. These ties can not be held responsible for impacting all types of firm behaviors, but past research suggests that strategic relationships are influential with respect to a set of behaviors related to the nature of these linkages. Therefore, strategic alliances are inter-organizational linkages across which firms (or stakeholders) influence one another. Using Freeman's language, they are ties through which stakeholders can "affect and are affected by" the focal firm.

The generalizability of the study to other stakeholder types and relationships is a concern because the selection of stakeholders and relationships is an exclusionary process. Stakeholder networks based on strategic alliances are relevant to two categories of stakeholders: those affected by the focal firm, and those who affect, and are affected, by the focal firm. Calton's (1993) examination of broad and limited views of stakeholders leads to a three-group categorization: (1) those affected by the organization, (2) those affecting the organization, and (3) those affecting and affected by the organization. Stakeholder networks comprised of strategic alliances among firms in the same industry involve actors who are capable of affecting and are affected by each other. However, these actors are not dependent stakeholders (Mitchell, Agle, and Wood, 1997)–those affected by, but which cannot affect the organization–because they do have the power to influence the focal organization.

Thus, the present study represents stakeholders and relationships characterized in Calton's latter two categories, and generalizations from this study should not be expanded to include stakeholder interactions involving purely dependent, non-influential stakeholders, such as non-profit organizations (e.g., soup kitchens) which rely on charitable donations from other social actors. However, stakeholder studies and theories focusing on the more influential stakeholders are relevant to how these vulnerable stakeholders behave. Frooman (1999) illustrates that stakeholders who are not capable of directly affecting the focal organization can use "indirect" strategies, thereby influencing other stakeholders who have the power to affect the focal organization. Similarly, Mitchell, Agle, and Wood (1997) suggest that "dependent" stakeholders rely on the advocacy of more powerful stakeholders to put forward their claims on the focal organization. Thus, insights gained from studying the interaction of influential stakeholders is meaningful for understanding how the "affected by" group of stakeholders can and should tap into the structure of stakeholder influences via other actors.

Data Collection

The two independent variables–density of the network structure and the centrality of the actors–are descriptive properties of the networks. To construct the steel and semiconductor industries' strategic alliance networks, I replicated Hagedoorn (1993) and Hagedoorn and Schakenraad's (1994) relational data technique, which has recently gained popularity in management research (Gulati, 1995; Madhavan, 1996). Relational data were collected primarily from published reports of alliance formation. These sources included newspapers, trade publications, business-related magazines, and associated databases.[1]

Measures

Construction of Social Network Matrices

To calculate structural measures, symmetric (non-directional), binary tie (i.e., "1" for a tie; "0" for no tie) matrices were constructed (Scott, 1991; Wasserman and Faust, 1994). Unlike directional ties, such as resource exchanges, which flow in one direction–from actor A to actor B–the strategic alliance ties in this study were non-direction relations and the matrices constructed from these ties were symmetrical. That is, the value in cell C_{ij} was also assigned to cell C_{ji}.

Network Measures

The structural variables in this study, network density and betweenness centrality, were computed using UCINET IV (Borgatti, Everett, and Freeman, 1992). To calculate unique densities for firms in both the semiconductor and steel industries, each network was dissected into smaller, egocentric networks for each firm. From each egocentric network, local densities were measured. Local density examines the interconnectedness of relationships among a focal firm and its direct partners. That is, it focused on a subset of relationships in the overall network and consists of a focal organization and all other actors who have a relationship with the focal firm. Scott (1991) suggests that this procedure is necessary when the study focuses on particular points or nodes in the network, as does the present study. In contrast, for a study examining system-level behaviors, network measures should be based on the structure of the overarching network.

Furthermore, the focal firm and its relationships were excluded from the local density calculations. "In an egocentric network it is usual to disregard the focal agent and his or her direct contacts, concentrating only on the links which exist among these contacts" (Scott, 1991: 75). The theory underlying this study dictated that this approach be adopted. It was the density among the set of stakeholders that was key to their ability to influence the focal organization. The focal firm and its relationships were not relevant to the density construct described in the theory. Thus, for the purposes of this study, a firm's density was measured as the number of existing ties in the ego network (other than those involving the focal organization), divided by the total possible number of ties among its stakeholders if each stakeholder were tied to every other stakeholder.

Centrality represented the degree to which a firm was situated on the paths connecting all other pairs of actors in their network. For example, actor i's centrality was calculated by totaling the number of geodesic paths linking actors j and k that actor i fell on, divided by the total number of geodesic paths linking actors j and k. Actor i's centrality was obtained by aggregating this value for all pairs of actors j and k, then normalizing the total.

Dependent variable
A survey instrument was employed to collect data on the degree to which organizations in the network adopted the four behavioral types: compromiser, commander, subordinate and solitarian. Managers from each network's member organizations were mailed a questionnaire. Each respondent was asked to answer questions, based on a Lickert scale, regarding a partner firm's behaviors. The questions were specific about the partner's treatment of the respondent's firm in their strategic alliance. Respondents were asked to provide these data for more than one partner. (Space for data on five partners was provided in the questionnaire.) In the operationalization of the dependent variable, the range of behaviors under study was narrowed to actions relevant to the interaction of strategic partners with one another. For H5 and H6, the dependent variable, financial performance, was operationalized using return on assets (ROA).

Ninety-three of 133 firms in the semiconductor network were surveyed. The remaining firms were excluded because there was evidence that the targeted respondents did not conduct their business communications in English. I feared that asking these managers to answer the survey in English or translating the survey would introduce significant errors in the data. Thirty-six semiconductor firms returned completed questionnaires, but six questionnaires were excluded from analysis, giving an adjusted response rate of 32 percent. In the steel industry, seventy-nine out of the network of 138 firms were mailed questionnaires. Thirty-one completed questionnaires were received, for a response rate of 39 percent.

Control Variable
Given that the dependent variables are related to how firms manage or "treat" their partners, a potential confounding factor is firm size. It could be argued that relatively large firms engage in resistance-type behaviors more often than smaller firms because they are likely to have access to many other substitute relationships and are less dependent on any one relationship (Pfeffer and Salancik, 1978). Furthermore, large firms will likely have more slack resources available and will therefore be able to resist stakeholder pressures even if structural conditions predict compliance. Thus, to examine the unique effects of density and centrality on firms' resistance behavior, it is important to control the effect of firm size. Firm size was measured as the natural logarithm of total assets. In addition, a dummy variable (i.e., "1" or "0") was used to control the effect a firm's industry type had on its financial performance and how it treated its stakeholders.

Analyses and Results
A variance-covariance approach to repeated measures ANOVA was employed because, in some cases, respondents (who provided observations on multiple partners) were captured in the data more than once. This statistical procedure provided a method for assessing whether responses made by the same firm were correlated.

Moreover, an exploratory approach to the data, rather than a strict hypothesis-testing process, was pursued because the theory and variables utilized in this study were relatively new, and therefore lacked a strong precedent. Consequently, regression analyses were performed on specific components of the data to provide further insight into the conclusions reached from the ANOVA analyses.

I performed a factor analysis of the questionnaire items to determine if the four behavioral variables–compromiser, subordinate, commander and solitarian–were independent of one another. Four factors were derived from a principal components factor analysis, and the results suggest that the items capture four independent variables, which match the four underlying theoretical constructs.

Table 1:   ANOVA Results

Variables	Commander	Solitarian	Compromiser	Subordinate
Density	-0.025***	-0.014*	0.006	0.014*
Centrality	0.021	0.127*	-0.08**	-0.05**
Firm Size	0.19**	0.027	-0.17**	-0.04

*p<.10, **p<.05, ***p<.01

Primary Analyses

Table 1 summarizes the results generated from the variance-covariance approach to repeated measures analysis (ANOVA). Four models were created to examine the predictions regarding the impact that density and centrality had on each behavioral type (outcome variables). The findings strongly support (p< .01) the hypothesis that density is negatively related to commander behavior (H5a) and there is moderate support (p< .10) for the hypothesized relationships between density and subordinate behavior (H4a) and density and solitarian behavior (H6a). However, density was not significantly related to compromiser behavior (H3a).

The findings also lend support to H3b and H4b (p< .05) because centrality was negatively and significantly related to compromiser and subordinate behavior (p< .05). However, although the relationship between centrality and commander behavior was in the expected direction, it was not significant (H5b). Interestingly, the findings show moderate support (p< .10) for the relationship between centrality and solitarian behavior (H6b). This relationship, however, contradicts the predicted direction.

In addition to the hypothesis-testing procedures above, several regression procedures were performed to supplement the findings and to assess H1, H2, H7 and H8. In H1 and H2, I predict that density is negatively related and centrality is positively related to an organization's resistance to stakeholder pressures. Using the net resistance measure–calculated by subtracting the subordinate scale from the commander scale–as the proxy for an organization's degree of resistance, regression results suggest that density and centrality are significantly related to resistance.

Table 2 summarizes the regression findings involving net resistance as the dependent variable. The independent variables were added in a step procedure so that the cumulative explained variance could be better understood. First, in Model I, the control variable (firm size), is the single variable in the regression, which yields $R^2 = .07$. In Model II, firm centrality is added to the analysis and, as a result, an additional 9 percent of the variance is explained (i.e., $R^2 = .16$). Density and firm size serve as the independent variables in Model III, yielding $R^2 = .17$. In Model IV, firm size, density and cen-

Table 2: Regression Analysis

Independent Variables		Model I Firm Size	Model II Firm size, centrality	Model III Firm size, density	Model IV Firm size, centrality, density	ROA
Constant	B	-6.51	-3.53	-4.8	-2.15	0.35
	SE	3.24	3.43	3.18	3.34	0.13
Size	B	0.27*	0.12	0.24	0.09	-0.017
	SE	0.14	0.16	0.14	0.15	0.005
	Beta (β)	0.27	0.12	0.24	0.09	-0.26
Industry	B	0.007	-0.18	-0.9	-1.01*	-0.10***
	SE B	0.51	0.5	0.62	0.6	0.02
	Beta (β)	0.002	-0.05	-0.25	-0.29	-0.66
Centrality	B		0.13**		0.12**	0.002
	SE B		0.06		0.06	0.002
	Beta (β)		0.32		0.3	0.11
Density	B			-0.03**	-0.03**	-0.002***
	SE B			0.01	0.01	0.005
	Beta (β)			-0.4	-0.37	-0.65
R^2		0.07	0.16	0.17	0.24	0.33
R^2 change			0.09	0.01	0.07	

*p<.10, **p<.05, ***p<.01

trality are incorporated and $R^2 = .24$, which provides an additional 8 percent and 7 percent of the variance explained in Models II (i.e., $R^2 = .16$) and III (i.e., $R^2 = .17$), respectively. Furthermore, the data for Model IV support H1, density is negatively related to resistance ($\beta = -.37$, p<.05); and H2, centrality is positively related to resistance ($\beta = .3$, p<.05). In addition, the regression findings suggest that density is strongly related to financial performance, measured as ROA (p<.01). Centrality was not significantly related to financial performance. Therefore the data support H7 but not H8.

Conclusions

Overall, the findings support many of the hypotheses tested and provide initial support for the claim that relational context is meaningful in understanding organization-stakeholder interactions. More specifically, the density of a stakeholder network and the focal organization's position in the network affect how the focal organization will treat its stakeholders. The data suggest that density negatively affects the focal organization's use of commander behaviors. Firms operating in dense stakeholder networks are less likely to manage their stakeholders by controlling and dominating the

Timothy J. Rowley

relationship than firms in sparsely connected networks. The findings suggest that centrality negatively affects compromiser and subordinate behaviors. Thus, firms occupying peripheral positions in their stakeholder networks are more likely to cooperate with their stakeholders–negotiate with, and acquiesce to, their stakeholders–than firms situated in central positions.

These findings have implications for corporate social performance (CSP) research. The behavioral types identified in this study represent one measure of CSP. Waddock and Graves (1997) argue that the stakeholder model of CSP, *how organizations treat their stakeholders*, is one approach for measuring CSP, which meets Jones' (1995) challenge to broaden the construct to include multiple stakeholders. The study herein provides a means for assessing how firms treat their stakeholders. The four behaviors vary in the degree to which an organization cooperates with its stakeholders. While commanders dominate their stakeholders and solitarians conceal their activities, compromisers and subordinates are more cooperative, attempting to negotiate and comply, respectively, with their stakeholders. The study's results provide evidence that firms surrounded by densely connected sets of stakeholders are less likely to exhibit non-cooperative behavior (attempt to resist or dominate their stakeholders) than firms operating in a sparsely connected stakeholder network. Thus, these findings suggest that firms in highly dense stakeholder networks are likely to exhibit higher levels of CSP than firms situated in sparse networks.

Tim Rowley (*rowley@mgmt.utoronto.ca*) is Assistant Professor in Strategic Management and Business Ethics at the Joseph L. Rotman School of Management at the University of Toronto, ON, M5S 3E6. This paper is based on his Ph.D. dissertation research, *Moving beyond dyadic ties: A network theory of stakeholder influences*, completed at the Joseph M. Katz Graduate School of Business, University of Pittsburgh. His advisory committee was chaired by Barry Mitnick.

---

[1]   Details on the data collection will be found in Rowley, T., Behrens, D., and Krackhardt, D. Redundant governance structures: An analysis of structural and relational embeddedness in the steel and semiconductor industries. Accepted for publication in *Strategic Management Journal; Networks Special Issue 1999*.

References

Allen, M.P. 1982. The identification of interlock groups in large corporate networks: Convergent validation using divergent techniques. *Social Networks*, 4: 349-366.

Ansoff, I. 1965. *Corporate strategy*. New York: McGraw Hill.

Borgatti, M.G., Jones, C., and Everett, M.G. 1992. *UCINET IV Version 1.0 reference manual*. Columbia: Analytical Technologies.

Brass, D.J., and Burkhardt, M.E. 1993. Potential power and power use: An investigation of structure and behavior. *Academy of Management Journal*, 36 (3): 441-47.

Burt, R.S. 1983. *Corporate profits and cooptation: Networks of market constraint and directorate ties in the American economy*. New York: Academic Press.

Calton, J.M. 1993. What is at stake in the stakeholder model? In *Business and society in a changing world order*, ed. D.C. Ludwig: 101-127. Lewiston: Edwin Mellen Press.

Contractor, F., and Lorange, P. 1988. Why should firms cooperate? The strategy and economics basis for cooperative ventures. In *Cooperative strategies in international business*, ed. F. Contractor and P. Lorange: 3-30. Lexington, MA: Lexington Books.

Freeman, L.C. 1979. Centrality in social networks: I. Conceptual clarifications. *Social Networks* 1: 215-239.

Freeman, R.E. 1984. *Strategic management: A stakeholder approach*. Boston: Pitman.

Frooman, J. 1999. Stakeholder influence strategies. *Academy of Management Review*, 24 (2): 191-205.

Galaskiewicz, J., and Wasserman, S. 1989. Mimetic processes within an interorganizational field: An empirical test. *Administrative Science Quarterly*, 34 (3): 454-479.

Gulati, R. 1995. Social structure and alliance formation: A longitudinal analysis. *Administrative Science Quarterly*, 40 (4) (Dec.): 619-652.

Hagedoorn, J. 1993. Understanding the rationale of strategic technology partnering: Interorganizational modes of cooperation and sectoral differences. *Strategic Management Journal*, 14 (5) (July): 371-385.

Hagedoorn, J., and Schakenraad, J. 1994. The effect of strategic technology alliances on company performance. *Strategic Management Journal*, 15 (4) (May): 291-309.

Jacobs, D. 1974. Dependency and vulnerability: An exchange approach to the control of organizations. *Administrative Science Quarterly*, 19 (1) (Mar.): 45-59.

Jones, T.M. 1995. Instrumental stakeholder theory: A synthesis of ethics and economics. *Academy of Management Review* 20 (2): 404-437.

Kilduff, M., and Krackhardt, D. 1994. Bringing the individual back in: A structural analysis of the internal market for reputation in organizations. *Academy of Management Journal*, 37 (1): 87-108.

Laumann, E.O., and Pappi, F.U. 1976. *Networks of collective action: A perspective on community influence systems*. New York: Academic Press.

Levine, J.H. 1972. The sphere of influence. *American Sociological Review*, 37: 14-27.

Madhavan, R. 1996. *Strategic flexibility and performance in the global steel industry*. Doctoral dissertation, Katz Graduate School of Business, University of Pittsburgh.

Meyer, J.W., and Rowan, B. 1977. Institutional organizations: Formal structures as myth and ceremony. *American Journal of Sociology*, 83 (2): 340-363.

Mintz, B., and Schwartz, M. 1981. The structure of intercorporate unity in American business. *Social Problems*, 29 (1): 87-103.

Mintz, B., and Schwartz, M. 1985. *The power structure of American business*. Chicago: University of Chicago Press.

Mintzberg, H. 1983. *Power in and around organizations.* Englewood Cliffs, NJ: Prentice-Hall.

Mitchell, R.K., Agle, B.R., and Wood, D.J. 1997. Toward a theory of stakeholder identification and salience: Defining the principle of who and what really counts. *Academy of Management Review,* 22 (4): 853-886.

Oliver, C. 1988. The collective strategy framework: An application to competing predictions of isomorphism. *Administrative Science Quarterly,* 33 (4) (Dec.): 543-561.

Oliver, C. 1991. Strategic responses to institutional processes. *Academy of Management Review,* 16 (1): 145-179.

Pfeffer, J., and Salancik, G.R. 1978. *The external control of organizations: A resource dependence perspective.* New York: Harper and Row.

Powell, W.W. 1988. Institutional effects on organizational structure and performance. In *Institutional patterns and organizations: Culture and environment,* ed. L.G. Zucker: 115-136. Cambridge, MA: Ballinger.

Rowley, T.J. 1997. Moving beyond dyadic ties: A network theory of stakeholder influences. *Academy of Management Review,* 22 (4) (Oct.): 887-91.

Scott, J. 1991. *Social network analysis: A handbook.* Thousand Oaks, CA: Sage.

Waddock, S.A., and Graves, S.B. 1997. Quality of management and quality of stakeholder relations. *Business & Society,* 36 (3): 250-279.

Wasserman, S., and Faust, K. 1994. *Social network analysis: Methods and applications.* New York: Cambridge.

Williamson, O. 1970. *Corporate control and business behavior: An inquiry into the effects of organization form on enterprise behavior.* Englewood Cliffs, NJ: Prentice-Hall.

Wood, D.J. 1994. Essay. In The Toronto conference: Reflections on stakeholder theory, ed. T.M. Jones. *Business & Society* 33 (1): 101-105.

Part 2

Management Processes

A Report on Stakeholder Attributes and Salience, Corporate Performance, and CEO Values

Bradley R. Agle, University of Pittsburgh
Ronald K. Mitchell, University of Victoria
Jeffrey A. Sonnenfeld, Chief Executive Leadership Institute

Introduction

In an attempt to improve our collective understanding of what Freeman (1994) called "the principle of who or what really counts," Mitchell, Agle, and Wood (1997) offered a theory of stakeholder identification and salience that suggests that managers' perceptions of three key stakeholder attributes—power, legitimacy, and urgency—affect stakeholder salience: the degree to which managers give priority to competing stakeholder claims. This study, summarized only briefly here, empirically tested Mitchell and colleagues' (1997) model as it applies to specific decisions made by chief executive officers (CEOs). Detailed background, methods, and analysis sections can be found in Agle, Mitchell, and Sonnenfeld (1999).

Leaders, especially the CEOs of business organizations, imprint their firms with their own values (Wally and Baum, 1994), which then become manifest in decision processes (Keeney, 1992; Norburn, 1989) that lead to stakeholder salience and corporate social performance (Carroll, 1979; Waddock and Graves, 1997a; Wood, 1991). We therefore studied CEOs' perceptions as important managerial outcomes described by the theory stated above, taking their values into account as Mitchell and colleagues suggested (1997: 871). Our study followed the "principles, processes, performance" logic suggested by Wood (1991: 693) as a straightforward way to examine the effects of CEOs' perceptions of stakeholder attributes on stakeholder salience and corporate performance.

Theory and Hypotheses

Our research model (Figure 1) is based upon Mitchell and colleagues' (1997: 873) proposition that stakeholder salience will be positively related to the cumulative number of stakeholder attributes—power, legitimacy, and urgency–perceived by managers to be present. Since these authors also argued that managerial characteristics are likely to moderate the attribute-salience relationship, and because the salience-performance link is implicit in their theory, we included CEO values as a moderating variable in the model and included several performance variables as outcomes.

To facilitate a faithful test of the model as proposed, we accept the Mitchell, Agle, and Wood (1997) definitions of the attributes of power, legitimacy, and urgency. And, we assume that:

- Stakeholder *power* exists where one social actor, A, can get another social actor, B, to do something that B would not have otherwise done (Dahl, 1957; Pfeffer, 1981; Weber, 1947).
- Stakeholder *legitimacy* is a generalized perception or assumption that the actions of an entity are desirable, proper, or appropriate within some socially constructed system of norms, values, beliefs, and definitions (Suchman, 1995; Weber, 1947).
- Stakeholder *urgency* is a multidimensional notion that includes both criticality and temporality, with a stakeholder claim considered to be urgent both when it is important and when delay in paying attention to it is unacceptable (Mitchell and Agle, 1997; Mitchell, Agle, and Wood, 1997).

We also accept Mitchell and colleagues' (1997: 854) definition of stakeholder salience as the degree to which managers give priority to competing stakeholder claims. However, their model of stakeholder salience was defined in terms of managerial perceptions, which necessitates further discussion. In their first proposition, those authors suggest that stakeholder salience is positively related to the cumulative number of the three variable attributes, power, legitimacy, and urgency, that are "*perceived* by managers to be present" (1997: 873; emphasis added). Further, Freeman (1984) observed that managers' priority perceptions may attach to stakeholder groups as well as to specific stakeholder claims. And, in addition to arguing that stakeholder attributes function as variables, not as steady states, and can change for any particular group or stakeholder-manager relationship, Mitchell, Agle, and Wood (1997: 868) argued that the existence (or the degree present) of each attribute as a matter of managerial perception is a reality constructed over time rather than an objective reality. Unfortunately, although the foregoing points draw attention to the role of perception, they do not constitute sufficient theoretical justification for why salience should be influenced by managerial perceptions. Social cognition theory and organization theory can provide the required explanations.

Social cognition theory, as an attempt to account for how people understand themselves and others, offers an explanation of how human cognitive

Bradley R. Agle, Ronald K. Mitchell, and Jeffrey A. Sonnenfeld

Figure 1: Research Model

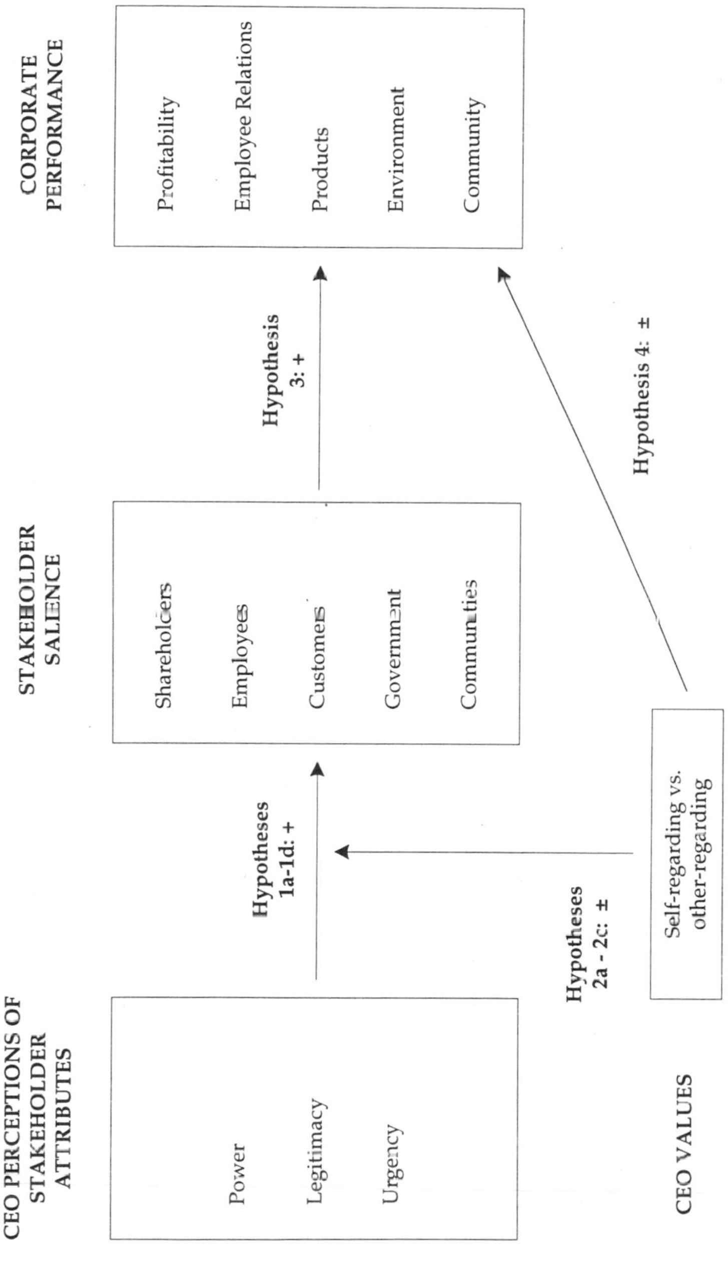

CEO PERCEPTIONS OF STAKEHOLDER ATTRIBUTES	STAKEHOLDER SALIENCE	CORPORATE PERFORMANCE
Power	Shareholders	Profitability
Legitimacy	Employees	Employee Relations
Urgency	Customers	Products
	Government	Environment
	Communities	Community

Hypotheses 1a-1d: +

Hypothesis 3: +

Hypotheses 2a - 2c: ±

Hypothesis 4: ±

CEO VALUES

Self-regarding vs. other-regarding

(Source: Agle, Mitchell, Sonnenfeld, 1999: 508.)

processes such as attention, person memory, and social inference affect outcomes of interest (Fiske and Taylor, 1984). Therefore, when we applied the general social cognition model to the stakeholder case, we expected stakeholder salience to be highest when both selectivity and intensity–the precursors of attention–were high, which provides a theoretical reason for the expectations proposed by Mitchell and his coauthors (1997). Hence, social cognition theory suggests that as the stakeholder attributes of power, legitimacy, and urgency cumulate in the mind of a manager, selectivity is enhanced, intensity is increased, and higher salience of the stakeholder group is the likely result.

Organization theory suggests that the cumulating of stakeholder attributes in the organizational setting might enhance the selectivity and intensity judgments (perceptions) of managers through the domination, differentiation, and/or novelty of one stakeholder compared to another, which in turn might affect stakeholder salience. Organizations "reconcile divergent interests" (Hill and Jones, 1992: 134), to accomplish an "interlocking of the behaviors of the various participants that comprise the organization" (Pfeffer and Salancik, 1978: 258), and to facilitate "aspiration-level adjustments" (Cyert and March, 1963: 38) that might be termed responses to "urgency" in Mitchell, Agle, and Wood (1997) terminology. We therefore had the following expectations for CEOs, stated as the following hypotheses (H):

H1a: The stakeholder attribute of power will be positively related to the stakeholder salience of shareholders, employees, customers, government, and communities.

H1b: The stakeholder attribute of legitimacy will be positively related to the stakeholder salience of shareholders, employees, customers, government, and communities.

H1c: The stakeholder attribute of urgency will be positively related to the stakeholder salience of shareholders, employees, customers, government, and communities.

And, since Mitchell and his coauthors (1997) suggested that stakeholder salience will be positively related to the cumulative number of stakeholder attributes–power, legitimacy, and urgency–perceived to be present, we also expected that for CEOs:

H1d: The cumulative number of the stakeholder attributes of power, legitimacy, and urgency will be positively related to the stakeholder salience of shareholders, employees, customers, government, and communities.

Bradley R. Agle, Ronald K. Mitchell, and Jeffrey A. Sonnenfeld

CEO Values and Stakeholder Salience

However, notwithstanding the direct effect of stakeholder attributes on salience, Mitchell and colleagues (1997) argued that the characteristics of managers are likely to moderate stakeholder salience. We therefore suggest that CEOs' values (Hambrick and Mason, 1984) are a primary characteristic that influence their perceptions of the attributes that lead to stakeholder salience. Thus, as Mitchell, Agle, and Wood (1997: 871) argue, the stakeholders that receive priority from management will be those whom managers–especially CEOs–perceive as highly salient.

Accordingly, we expected that, in general:

H2a: CEO values will affect CEO perceptions of power, legitimacy, and urgency and thus will be related to the stakeholder salience of shareholders, employees, customers, government, and communities.

Further, because CEO values are expected to vary on a continuum anchored at one end by profit maximization-firm-centered values and at the other by other-regarding-system-centered values (Wood, 1994), we specifically expected that:

H2b: CEO other-regarding values will affect CEO perceptions of power, legitimacy, and urgency and thus will be positively related to stakeholder salience for non-shareholders (employees, customers, government, and communities).

H2c: CEO other-regarding values will affect CEO perceptions of power, legitimacy, and urgency and thus will be negatively related to stakeholder salience for shareholders.

Stakeholder Salience and Corporate Performance

Within the stakeholder literature exists the highly appealing idea that paying attention to stakeholders is also good business (Jones, 1995). Recently, an explicit link has been suggested between stakeholder theory and corporate social performance (CSP), on the basis of the argument that CSP is all about the relationships between a firm and its stakeholders–with the quality of these relationships fundamentally defining the quality of a company's corporate social performance (Waddock and Graves, 1997b). Hence, we expected that:

H3: Stakeholder salience as perceived by CEOs will be positively related to corporate performance.

In hypothesizing this relationship, however, we were not unaware of the difficulties associated with its testing. Several variables that could not be included in our study might also affect the results. For example, the influence of CEOs on outcomes might not be as great as expected for a number of reasons, including, for example, inflated expectations on our part. (See Agle, Mitchell, and Sonnenfeld (1999) for details.)

CEO Values and Corporate Performance

Two contrasting points of view explain some of the variations in CEO values as they affect corporate performance. One end of the spectrum is anchored by an emphasis on the firm as the center of a stakeholder nexus. This shareholder-profit maximization focus emphasizes managing stakeholder relationships for the firm's and its managers' benefit. The other end of this values spectrum is anchored by what we have referred to above as an other-regarding-system-centered view of relationships with stakeholders. Thus, it was reasonable to expect that:

H4a: CEO values will be related to corporate performance.

H4b: CEO other-regarding values will be positively related to corporate social performance variables (employee relations, product innovation/ safety, environmental stewardship, and community relations).

Although we expected a clear relationship between CEO other-regarding values and these CSP variables, the relationship between CEO values and corporate financial performance is not as clear. Conventional wisdom (Jensen, 1988) suggests that corporations will perform better to the extent that CEOs concentrate on narrow profit maximization. This notion has been challenged by Clarkson (1988) and Miles (1987), whose research suggests that CEOs with other-regarding-system-centered values lead organizations that outperform their competitors on financial performance measures. Thus, to further test the conventional wisdom that narrow, firm-centered values will lead to greater financial performance, we hypothesized that:

H4c: CEO other-regarding values will be negatively related to the profitability component of corporate performance.

Methods

We developed a unique dataset on the three stakeholder attributes, salience, CEO values, and performance, and used it to test the hypotheses. The dataset was developed from primary data gathered in 1997 and 1998 using surveys sent to 588 CEOs at firms in the Kinder, Lydenberg, Domini, and Company (KLD) database. Eighty CEOs returned completed surveys, for a 13.6 percent response rate. Response rates for CEOs are notoriously low, and our response rate for the KLD sample was normal for this population (Friedman and Singh, 1989).

The survey instrument asked respondents to choose answers from seven-point Likert scales (1, strongly disagree, to 7, strongly agree). Questions on stakeholder attributes were adapted from research by Mitchell and Agle (1997); survey instruments developed by Rokeach (1972) and Aupperle (1984) were adapted to measure values and attitudes toward corporate social responsibility (CSR).

Data Analysis

This section provides a very simplified outline of the data analysis. Full details can be found in Agle, Mitchell, and Sonnenfeld (1999).

Various statistical tests were performed on the data. Table 1 provides the means, standard deviations, and correlations for the variables used to test hypotheses H1a to H1c and H2a to H2c.

To test H1a to H1c, we performed analyses for each of the five stakeholder groups, regressing the three stakeholder attributes (power, legitimacy, and urgency) against stakeholder salience. To comply with the assumptions of regression analysis, we transformed the dependent variable, salience, for normalcy in the data for three groups, shareholders, employees, and customers. We used the reflective inverse transformation suggested by Tabachnick and Fidell (1996) for a J-shaped distribution skewed to the left.

To test H1d, we used a simplified form of the mathematical decision structure devised by Mitchell and Agle (1997: 368) to help researchers quantify the absence or presence of variables. As Mitchell and Agle suggested (1997: 370), we quantified the absence/presence of the stakeholder attributes to correspond to the absence/presence conditions existing in each case to form a basic interval scale (Nunnally, 1978:16). We then established a threshold value for each attribute, using (in the absence of any data in the literature) the mean value on that attribute in our sample. The cumulative number of stakeholder attributes above the threshold level for each stakeholder was then regressed against the salience of that stakeholder.

To test H2a, H2b, and H2c, we performed a moderated regression analysis on each stakeholder group using CEO assessments of the three attributes, power, legitimacy, and urgency; our two measures of CEO values; and the interaction of CEO attributes and CEO values on stakeholder salience. H3 was tested in two different ways. Firstly, we examined simple Pearson correlations to determine if significant relationships existed between the salience of each particular stakeholder group and performance. Secondly, we combined the data and regressed each stakeholder group salience rating against the matching performance rating (Wood and Jones, 1995). Thus, employee salience was matched with the KLD employee relations score, shareholder salience was matched with return on equity (ROE) (both return on assets [ROA] and ROE in the first analysis), community salience was matched with the KLD community relations measure, customer salience was matched with

Table 1: Means, Standard Deviations, and Correlations of Stakeholder Attributes, Stakeholder salience, and CEO Values

Variable	Mean	s.d.	1	2	3	4	5	6	7	8	9	10	11	12	13	14	15	16	17	18	19	20	21	22	23	24	25
1. Shareholder power	6.1	0.9																									
2. Shareholder legitimacy	6.2	1.1	0.13																								
3. Shareholder urgency	5.2	1.8	0.37***	0.39***																							
4. Shareholder salience	6.3	0.8	0.29**	0.31***	0.45***																						
5. Employee power	5.6	1.0	0.33***	0.26**	0.19	0.08																					
6. Employee legitimacy	6.1	0.9	0.60	0.38***	0.19*	0.21*	0.21*																				
7. Employee urgency	5.1	1.4	0.27**	0.06	0.53***	0.15	0.20*	0.12																			
8. Employee salience	6.4	0.6	0.20*	0.19*	0.12	0.32***	0.36***	0.36***	0.13																		
9. Customer power	6.3	0.9	0.22*	0.05	-0.04	-0.08	0.33***	0.19	-0.06	0.23**																	
10. Customer legitimacy	6.3	1.1	0.19	0.47***	0.20*	0.07	0.20*	0.33***	0.07	0.23**	0.44***																
11. Customer urgency	5.5	1.5	0.10	0.27	0.37***	0.10	0.01	0.15	0.29**	0.10	0.30***	0.33***															
12. Customer salience	6.6	0.5	0.01	0.10	-0.04	0.03	0.15	0.18	-0.07	0.34***	0.60***	0.57***	0.35***														
13. Government power	5.9	1.1	0.14	0.00	-0.17	0.14	0.08	-0.05	0.02	-0.01	0.22	0.17	-0.13	0.11													
14. Government legitimacy	4.1	1.7	0.03	0.07	0.04	0.00	0.13	0.34***	0.16	-0.04	0.07	0.00	0.15	0.01	0.03												
15. Government urgency	3.9	1.8	0.20*	-0.03	0.01	0.00	0.18	0.16	0.27**	-0.03	0.12	0.04	0.35***	0.11	0.19*	0.21*											
16. Government salience	5.1	1.6	0.04	-0.06	-0.11	0.17	0.00	0.05	0.18	-0.03	-0.01	0.00	-0.04	0.04	0.29***	0.13	0.44***										
17. Community power	3.0	1.6	0.19*	0.00	0.00	-0.04	0.11	0.13	0.09	-0.03	0.14	0.01	0.18	0.06	0.08	0.25**	0.39***	0.23**									
18. Community legitimacy	4.4	1.4	0.17	0.09	0.18	-0.02	0.18	0.29**	0.12	0.02	0.23	0.07	0.23	0.16	0.05	0.45***	0.30***	0.31***	0.49***								
19. Community urgency	4.1	1.7	0.13	-0.03	0.15	0.14	-0.06	0.17	0.39***	-0.03	0.09	0.00	0.36***	0.04	0.01	0.28**	0.36***	0.36***	0.49***	0.32***							
20. Community salience	4.0	1.6	0.18	0.10	0.11	0.12	0.04	0.20	0.16	0.09	0.13	0.00	0.29***	0.11	0.05	0.23**	0.35***	0.42***	0.52***	0.63***	0.47***						
21. Values, Rokeach	4.2	0.9	-0.04	-0.17	0.00	0.08	0.03	0.17	0.03	0.19*	-0.24**	-0.15	-0.02	-0.14	0.08	0.20*	0.16	0.28**	0.21	0.34***	0.18	0.30***					
22. Values, Aupperle	-1.0	2.3	-0.16	-0.30***	-0.29***	-0.15	-0.14	0.02	-0.20*	0.06	-0.08	-0.11	-0.18	0.01	0.13	0.00	-0.05	0.10	-0.02	-0.03	0.07	0.03	0.38***				
23. CSR, economic	3.3	1.0	0.08	0.27**	0.26**	0.02	0.04	-0.04	0.18	-0.18	0.11	0.04	-0.18	0.01	-0.17	0.01	0.03	-0.13	0.00	-0.02	-0.03	-0.06	-0.37***	-0.87			
24. CSR, legal	2.7	0.7	0.00	0.04	-0.27**	0.10	0.01	-0.06	-0.25**	0.19	0.10	0.11	-0.02	0.25**	0.20*	-0.13	-0.07	0.02	-0.14	-0.06	-0.19*	-0.15	-0.02	0.16	-0.38***		
25. CSR, ethical	2.6	0.8	-0.19	-0.23	-0.24**	-0.24**	-0.20	0.00	-0.17	-0.07	-0.03	-0.15	-0.13	0.03	0.05	0.02	-0.06	0.03	-0.03	-0.08	0.09	-0.01	0.27**	0.84***	-0.48***	-0.12	
26. CSR, discretionary	1.1	0.7	0.09	-0.05	0.15	0.16	0.09	0.07	0.15	0.17	-0.14	0.04	0.00	-0.10	-0.02	0.03	0.08	0.18	0.18	0.22*	0.13	0.36***	0.20*	-0.11	-0.15	-0.32**	-0.37***

*p<.10, **p<.05, ***p<.01

(Source: Agle, Mitchell, Sonnenfeld, 1999: 516.)

Bradley R. Agle, Ronald K. Mitchell, and Jeffrey A. Sonnenfeld the KLD products measure, and government salience was matched with the KLD environment measure (see Agle, Mitchell, and Sonnenfeld (1999) for details). Finally, H4a to H4c were tested through a correlational analysis, with simple Pearson correlations showing the relationships between the various measures of CEO values, CSP variables, and financial performance variables.

Results

Statistical results of the hypothesis tests are found in Tables 1 through 3. The results presented in Tables 1 and 2 showed strong support for H1a to H1d, suggesting that the stakeholder attributes of power, legitimacy, and urgency are indeed related to stakeholder salience. Table 1 shows that shareholder salience is significantly related to shareholder power, legitimacy, and urgency (p<.05, .01, and .01, respectively); employee salience to employee power and legitimacy (both p<.01); customer salience to customer power, legitimacy, and urgency (all p<.01); government salience to government power and urgency (p<.05 and .01, respectively); and community salience to community power, legitimacy, and urgency (all p<.01). Table 2 presents the results of the regression analyses for individual attributes in its top half and results for cumulative attributes in its lower half. Effect sizes range from an adjusted R^2 value of .17 for employee salience to a value of .52 for customer salience in the individual attributes models, and from an adjusted R^2 value of .14 for employee salience to a value of .47 for shareholder salience in the cumulative attributes models.

Table 3 shows the results of moderated regression analyses testing H2a to H2c. The top half of the table shows a significant effect (p<.05) on employee salience for the interaction between CEOs' other-regarding values, as measured by the Rokeach instrument, and stakeholder attributes. The lower half shows a significant effect (p<.05) on customer salience for the interaction between other-regarding values, as measured by the Aupperle instrument, and stakeholder attributes. However, except for these findings, the overall pattern of results is one of non-significance. Thus, although two significant interaction effects were found, it appears that the majority of the evidence suggests that we retain the null hypothesis, that values have no moderating effect.

The results of the analysis used to test H3 and H4a to H4c, provided in detail in Mitchell, Agle, and Sonnenfeld (1999), are briefly outlined here. H3 states that stakeholder salience will be related to corporate performance. An overall regression analysis (not shown) using all ratings (n = 374) between a stakeholder group's salience and corporate outcome matched for that stakeholder group yielded no significant relationship. A significant (p<.05) correlation was found between community salience and community performance. Nevertheless, the general pattern of results does not allow us to reject the null hypothesis and, once again, this hypothesis–that there is no relationship between stakeholder salience and corporate performance–is retained.

Results showed slight support for H4a to H4c, suggesting a relationship between CEO values and corporate performance. There is a correlation approaching significance (p<.10) between CEO values, as measured by the Rokeach instrument, and community performance. A significant correlation (p<.01) is also seen between CSP discretion, as measured on the Aupperle scale, and community performance. However, the overall pattern of findings does not justify rejecting the null assumption for H4a to H4c, and therefore it is once again retained. Thus, no significant relationship was found between CEO values and corporate performance.

Discussion and Conclusion

The primary objective of this study was to test the theoretical model of stakeholder salience proposed by Mitchell and colleagues (1997). Our results confirmed this model. We found that in the minds of CEOs, the stakeholder attributes of power, legitimacy, and urgency are individually (with only two exceptions) and cumulatively (with no exception) related to stakeholder salience across all groups. This finding suggests that these stakeholder attributes do affect the degree to which top managers give priority to competing stakeholders.

Table 2:   *Results of Regression Analysis*

	Salience:	*Shareholder*	*Employee*	*Customer*	*Government*	*Community*
Variable						
Individual attributes						
Stakeholder power		0.16	0.25**	0.34***	0.30***	0.23**
Stakeholder legitimacy		0.18*	0.30***	0.46***	0.07	0.47***
Stakeholder urgency		0.40***	0.06	0.11	0.34***	0.17*
Adjusted R²		0.30***	0.17***	0.52***	0.23***	0.48***
F		11.15	5.83	26.39	8.23	22.72
n		73	73	72	72	71
Cumulative attributes						
Number of stakeholder attributes exceeding threshold		0.69***	0.38***	0.65***	0.41***	0.56***
Adjusted R²		0.47***	0.14***	0.42***	0.15***	0.30***
F		65.48	12.24	51.58	13.91	31.48
n		73	73	72	72	71

*p<.10, **p<.05, ***p<.01

(Source: Agle, Mitchell, Sonnenfeld, 1999: 519.)

    Bradley R. Agle, Ronald K. Mitchell, and Jeffrey A. Sonnenfeld

Table 3: Interaction Effects[a]

	Shareholders		Employees		Customers		Government		Community	
	Adjusted R²	ΔR²	Adjusted R²	ΔR²	Adjusted R²	ΔR²	Adjusted R²	ΔR²	Adjusted R²	ΔR²
CEO values, Rokeach										
Stakeholder power, legitimacy and urgency	0.29***		0.18***		0.52***		0.23***		0.46***	
CEO values, Rokeach	0.27	-0.02	0.25	0.07**	0.51	-0.01	0.24	0.01	0.45	-0.01
n	71		71		70		70		69	
CEO values, Aupperle										
Stakeholder power, legitimacy and urgency	0.30***		0.19***		0.52***		0.24***		0.48***	
CEO values, Aupperle	0.28	-0.01	0.2	0.01	0.57	0.04**	0.23	-0.01	0.46	-0.02
n	72		72		71		71		70	

[a] Because of missing data, a slight variation in *n* results in minor variations between Tables 2 and 3 in values of adjusted R^2.

*p<.10, **p<.05, ***p<.01

(Source: Agle, Mitchell, Sonnenfeld, 1999: 519.)

A secondary objective of the study was to test other relationships: the potentially moderating effect of CEO values on the attribute-salience and salience-performance links, and the effects of salience on performance. With a few minor exceptions, these tests showed few relationships among the variables as operationally defined. These findings suggest that much more work will be necessary before researchers will be able to fully understand these phenomena, and, as explained in more detail in Agle, Mitchell, and Sonnenfeld (1999), they suggest a continuing emphasis on normative stakeholder theory.

The capability of normative declarations to alter outcomes is well accepted. "We hold these truths to be self-evident . . . "; "inalienable rights, . . . life, liberty, . . . pursuit of happiness . . . " and similar statements contain within them social energy that inspires the mind, justifies new modes of thought, and enables change. In our study, we observed that the terms "stakeholder" and "really counting" are not yet synonymous. We suggest that without the persistent and persuasive linking of these terms in the normative discourse of our society, and without careful construction upon this foundation of a truly viable, rigorous alternative to the dominant view (Clarkson, 1995), the future of the corporation is uncertain.

We reason as follows: in our study, we saw that, at present, society does grant authority (legitimacy and power) to business leaders, shareholders, employees, and customers. And we are reminded of Davis's "iron law," which states that "in the long run, those who do not use power in a manner which society considers responsible will tend to lose it" (Davis, 1973: 314). It appears to us that after over thirty years of attention to the stakeholder concept, it is unlikely that either descriptive or instrumental discourse will generate the social energy necessary to forge an actual link between stakeholder salience and corporate social performance. Descriptive discourse describes a corporation as a constellation of cooperative and competitive interests possessing intrinsic value, while instrumental discourse establishes a framework for examining the connections between the practice of stakeholder management and the achievement of various corporate performance goals (Donaldson and Preston, 1995). As helpful as these aspects of stakeholder theory are in explaining "what is," normative discourse, we believe, must continue to be central to stakeholder theory and research. This is necessary if scholars want the theory to flourish and fulfill its aims as a theory of the firm–not the least of which is attending to the long-run interests of both the business corporation and the society that gives it life.

Bradley R. Agle *(agle@vms.cis.pitt.edu)* is an assistant professor at the Joseph M. Katz Graduate School of Business, University of Pittsburgh, Pittsburgh, PA 15260. He received his Ph.D. from the University of Washington. His research interests include strategic and moral leadership, stakeholder theory, values, corporate social responsibility, and religious influences on business.

Ronald K. Mitchell *(mitch@business.uvic.ca)* is an associate professor in the Faculty of Business at the University of Victoria, Victoria, BC V8W 2Y2. He received his Ph.D. from the University of Utah. His research interests focus on entrepreneurship–specifically, the study of expert information-processing theory, strategic management, and stakeholder theory as they apply to entrepreneurs, ventures, and the venturing environment.

Jeffrey A. Sonnenfeld *(jeffrey.sonnenfeld@yale.edu)* is the chairman and president of the Chief Executive Leadership Institute in Atlanta. He is also an adjunct professor of leadership at the Yale University School of Management, New Haven, CT 06520. He received his doctorate from Harvard University. His research interests focus upon chief executive leadership, the careers of top leaders, corporate social performance, corporate governance, and top management teams.

References

Agle, B.R., Mitchell, R.K., and Sonnenfeld, J.A. 1999. Who matters to CEOs?: An investigation of stakeholder attributes and salience, corporate performance, and CEO values. *Academy of Management Journal*, 42 (5) (Oct.) 1999: 507-525.

Aupperle, K.E. 1984. An empirical measure of corporate social orientation. *Research in Corporate Social Performance and Policy*, 6: 27-54.

Clarkson, M.B.E. 1988. Corporate social performance in Canada, 1976-86. *Research in Corporate Social Performance and Policy*, 10: 241-265.

Clarkson, M.B.E. 1995. A stakeholder framework for analyzing and evaluating corporate social performance. *Academy of Management Review*, 20 (1) (Jan.): 92-117.

Cohen, J. 1988. *Statistical power analysis for the behavioral sciences.* 2nd ed. New York: Academic Press.

Cyert, R.M., and March, J.G. 1963. *A behavioral theory of the firm.* Englewood Cliffs, NJ: Prentice-Hall.

Dahl, R.A. 1957. The concept of power. *Behavioral Science*, 2: 201-215.

Davis, K. 1973. The case for and against business assumption of social responsibilities. *Academy of Management Journal*, 16 (2): 312-322.

Donaldson, T., and Preston, L.E. 1995. The stakeholder theory of the corporation: Concepts, evidence and implications. *Academy of Management Review*, 20 (1): 65-91.

Fiske, S.T., and Taylor, S.E. 1984. *Social cognition.* Reading, MA: Addison-Wesley.

Freeman, R.E. 1984. *Strategic management: A stakeholder approach.* Boston: Pitman.

Freeman, R.E. 1994. The politics of stakeholder theory: Some future directions. *Business Ethics Quarterly*, 4 (4): 409-421.

Friedman, S.D., and Singh, H. 1989. CEO succession and stockholder reaction: The influence of organizational context and event content. *Academy of Management Journal*, 32 (4): 718-744.

Hair, J.F., Jr., Anderson, R.E., Tatham, R.L., and Black, W.C. 1995. *Multivariate data analysis*. 4th ed. Englewood Cliffs, NJ: Prentice-Hall.

Hambrick, D.C., and Mason, P.A. 1984. Upper echelons: The organization as a reflection of its top managers. *Academy of Management Review*, 9 (2): 193-206.

Hill, C.W.L., and Jones, T.M. 1992. Stakeholder-agency theory. *Journal of Management Studies*, 29 (2): 131-154.

Jensen, M.C., and Meckling, W.H. 1976. Theory of the firm: Managerial behavior, agency costs, and ownership structure. *Journal of Financial Economics*, 3 (4): 305-360.

Jones, T.M. 1995. Instrumental stakeholder theory: A synthesis of ethics and economics. *Academy of Management Review*, 20 (2): 404-437.

Keeney, R.L. 1992. *Value-focused thinking: A path to creative decision making*. Cambridge, MA: Harvard University Press.

Miles, R.H. 1987. *Managing the corporate social environment: A grounded theory*. Englewood Cliffs, NJ: Prentice-Hall.

Mitchell, R.K., and Agle, B.R. 1997. Stakeholder identification and salience: Dialogue and operationalization. In *Proceedings of the Eighth Annual Meeting of the International Association for Business and Society held in Destin, FL, 6-9 March 1997*, ed. J. Weber and K. Rehbein: 365-370.

Mitchell, R.K., Agle, B.R., and Wood, D.J. 1997. Toward a theory of stakeholder identification and salience: Defining the principle of who and what really counts. *Academy of Management Review*, 22 (4): 853-886.

Norburn, D. 1989. The chief executive: A breed apart. *Strategic Management Journal*, 10 (1): 1-15.

Nunnally, J. 1978. *Psychometrics*. New York: McGrawHill.

Pfeffer, J. 1981. *Power in organizations*. Marshfield, MA: Pitman.

Pfeffer, J., and Salancik, G.R. 1978. *The external control of organizations: A resource dependence perspective*. New York: Harper and Row.

Rokeach, M. 1972. *Beliefs, attitudes, and values: A theory of organization and change*. San Francisco: Jossey-Bass.

Suchman, M.C. 1995. Managing legitimacy: Strategic and institutional approaches. *Academy of Management Review*, 20 (3) (July): 571-610.

Tabachnick, B.G., and Fidell, L.S. 1996. *Using multivariate statistics*. 3rd ed. New York: Harper Collins.

Waddock, S.A., and Graves, S.B. 1997a. The corporate social performance-financial performance link. *Strategic Management Journal*, 18 (4): 303-319.

Waddock, S.A., and Graves, S.B. 1997b. Quality of management and quality of stakeholder relations. *Business & Society*, 36 (3): 250-279.

Wally, S., and Baum, J.R. 1994. Personal and structural determinants of the pace of strategic decision making. *Academy of Management Journal*, 37 (4): 923-940.

Weber, M. 1947. *The theory of social and economic organization*. New York: Free Press.

Wood, D.J. 1991. Corporate social performance revisited. *Academy of Management Review*, 16 (4): 691-718.

Wood, D.J. 1994. Essay. In The Toronto conference: Reflections on stakeholder theory, ed. T.M. Jones. *Business & Society* 33 (1): 101-105.

Wood, D.J., and Jones, R.E. 1995. Stakeholder mismatching: A theoretical problem in empirical research on corporate social performance. *International Journal of Organizational Analysis*, 3 (3): 229-267.

Defining "Community as Stakeholder" and "Community Stakeholder Management": A Theory Elaboration Study

Barbara W. Altman, Boston College and University of North Texas

Introduction

Throughout the stakeholder literature "community" is mentioned as one of a number of constituent groups to which corporations are responsible. The concept of community as stakeholder, however, lacks full definition. The sometimes stated, but often implied, meaning is the geographic locale of the corporation's facilities. This research project shows that this definition is no longer applicable in our current business climate, and provides little direction for community stakeholder management, the managerial extension of "community as stakeholder."

This study has three research objectives:

1. To define community as stakeholder by merging theoretical frameworks with new empirical data;
2. To develop a definition of community stakeholder management; and
3. To identify practical and theoretical applications for these definitions.

In this report, background is briefly provided on the increasing importance of the "community as stakeholder" in terms of two trends in corporate community practice.[1] These trends are then explained in terms of existing frameworks in the literatures of stakeholder theory, corporate social responsibility (CSR), and sociology. The gaps identified between theory and practice form the impetus for the current study: a qualitative investigation of community as stakeholder and community stakeholder management in firms from the petroleum and retail industries.

Background

Increasing Importance of Community Relations
Recent practitioner-oriented studies by major business consortia like the Conference Board (Alperson, 1995; Garone, 1995), and the Boston College Center for Corporate Community Relations (Litchfield, 1997) show that community issues have risen to high priority levels with corporate executives. Further, in a survey of the public affairs offices of major American corporations, Post and Griffin (1997) found that community relations was one of the three fastest growing areas of public affairs, with 23 percent of the companies surveyed having added a community relations office within the past four years.

Other recent studies document the business benefits of community involvement. Improved corporate reputation is mentioned most often (Fombrun, 1996; Smith, 1994; Tichy, McGill, and St. Clair, 1997), followed by improved employee morale, loyalty impacting productivity (Hanson et al., 1994; Tichy, McGill, and St. Clair, 1997), and the ability to preserve or enhance the company's license to operate (Burke, 1999).

While corporate executives and managers are placing a higher priority on community issues, they are finding them increasingly complex (Altman, 1996; Hanson, 1994; Waddock and Boyle, 1995; Tichy, McGill, and St. Clair, 1997). Waddock and Boyle (1995), in their study of trends in community relations, note the complexity of moving from a function focused on one "community," the headquarters community, to multiple "communities" in the global business environment. They also note a trend in community relations for increased democratization of decision-making to allow for increased employee and local involvement.

These studies are evidence that corporate managers and executives are evaluating what "community" is and what responsibility the corporation has towards it. Central to this evaluation are managers' and executives' concepts of community, community responsibility, and the corporate actions these necessitate. Some insights about these concepts are identified in the next sections from trends in community affairs practice and the literatures of stakeholder theory, corporate social responsibility, and sociology. The gaps remaining between theory and practice are addressed by research questions that form the basis of the current study.

Literature Review
The recent growth in community affairs functions is a response to two trends in corporate community practice. The first is a pressure to link community affairs to corporate strategy; the second is the increasing managerial complexity of responsibility to multiple "communities."

The first trend, associated with strategic pressures and motivational changes, may be driven by corporate re-engineering and downsizing. Community relations functions are being tied into corporate strategy, and are required to show measurable results. Smith (1994) points out that while the linkage between strategy and philanthropy has existed for some time, the linking of general community involvement (e.g., volunteerism) to corporate strategy is more recent. Tichy, McGill, and St. Clair (1997), for example, frame their collection of corporate citizenship studies in strategic terms. Waddock and Boyle (1995) and Altman (1996) discuss this trend as a move from a values-oriented approach to community relations to a strategic one.

These trends in corporate practice are at odds with theoretical frameworks. Practice trends are beginning to frame community involvement as economics-based, the stakeholder literature does not.

A core argument in stakeholder theory literature is that responsibility to the community stakeholder is moral, not economic. For instance, in their chronological overview of stakeholder definitions, Mitchell, Agle, and Wood (1997) identify a theoretical definition of "stakeholder as moral interest" in which the concept of community is consistently included. By contrast, another narrow category of "stakeholder as economic interest" does not always include the concept of community. Normative frameworks (Freeman 1998; Burton and Dunn, 1996; Carroll, 1991; Vidaver-Cohen, 1996) ground their work in the moral obligation of the firm to act responsibly toward its local communities and community groups.

Clarkson (1994, 1998) defines community as an "involuntary" stakeholder, one that is unknowingly exposed to risk. His work, coupled with Mitchell, Agle, and Wood's (1997) concept of salience, brings up an important point: individuals and community groups have not traditionally been considered powerful enough to be considered stakeholders. The normative portions of the stakeholder literature, such as Burton and Dunn's (1996) "caring" approach, have been more inclusive of the community as a stakeholder because the majority of community interests have not been covered in an economic stakeholder model.

The CSR literature has struggled with a similar argument about corporate responsibility being economic/social or strategy/values based. While the case has been made that the corporation and its communities interpenetrate over time (Post, 1978), the economic impact of that interplay has not been quantified. Newer work in corporate philanthropy (Smith, 1994) charts a movement toward strategic drivers. Corporate philanthropy has been in existence since early periods in American economic history (Heald, 1988; Sharfman, 1994) and while labeled a discretionary function of the firm (Carroll, 1979), in many communities it is an established and expected practice (Galasiewicz, 1985; Galasiewicz and Burt, 1991). Many studies have investigated the corporate motivations for philanthropy, noting a complex interplay of values, and institutional and strategic rationales (Burke et al.,

1986; Siegfried *et al.*, 1983; Useem, 1988, 1991).

Miles (1987), in a study of the insurance industry, used contingency theory (Chandler, 1962; Lawrence and Lorsch, 1967) to chart values and strategy as variables that determine the strategy and structure of the external affairs function. He found a contingent relationship between top management philosophy (values) and external affairs strategy; and business exposure (corporate strategy) and external affairs structure and processes. Some of these same elements are currently seen in managerial practice; therefore, Miles' research may provide a useful framework for studying community stakeholder management.

The second trend in corporate practice, the managing of multiple "communities," is rooted in definitional concepts of *community as stakeholder* and *community stakeholder management*. The linkage of the definitional component with the managerial component, as advocated in stakeholder theory, seems to be at work in current practice. The increasing complexity of community affairs stems from defining, and then taking action in, multiple "communities." In the past, as the philanthropy literature documents, corporate community involvement has been restricted primarily to the headquarters community.

Community is among a number of stakeholders commonly identified in the literature, yet its definitions are imprecise. Burton and Dunn (1996), for example, typically found the term used along with conceptually related terms like "general public," "public stakeholders," and the "natural environment," and concluded that treatment of community is "amorphous." They argue that money cannot be given to "the community": in practice, money in the form of taxes goes to the local government; money in the form of contributions goes to local non-profit organizations. Burton and Dunn further argue that lumping together, as a single entity, the many different groups and individuals that make up a geographic community, leads to abstractions inconsistent with Freeman's classic definition of "stakeholder", that is, "any group or individual who can affect or is affected by the achievement of the organization's objectives" (1984: 46). Freeman's definition commands recognition of all individuals within that population. Drawing on another definition of stakeholder, the contracts perspective, Burton and Dunn argue that it is impossible to have a real contact with "the community," although it is possible to have an implicit "social contract" (Donaldson and Preston, 1995).

The CSR and stakeholder literatures, therefore, assume a homogeneity that no longer exists in a diverse and global society. Recent works in the literature of sociology have struggled with defining community in an increasingly diverse society. Sociologists distinguish between a "gemeinschaft," meaning the traditional homogeneous community, and a "gesellschaft," meaning a broader view of urban societies (cities) with no moral or community base (Etzioni, 1992; Gardner, 1991; Selznick, 1992). Etzioni proposes that our society today is neither a *gemeinschaft* nor *gesellschaft*, but a mixture of the two. He advocates a concept of community that balances the need for diversity and unity, while not stifling the interests of sub-communities–a "new gemeinschaft" paradigm (Etzioni, 1992:122). This struggle to refine the definitions of *gemeinschaft* and *gesellschaft* also provides a promising framework for the current study. Management theorists should look for a similar path in defining "community as stakeholder": one that provides for the diversity of subgroups and multiple opinions within one locale, yet allows the identification of some homogeneity so that community stakeholder management is possible.

A gap between theory and practice in the existing stakeholder and CSR literatures is the lack of a managerial framework for corporate community action. Research on philanthropy provides some understanding of the contributions function, although this work may be outdated because it primarily applies to the headquarters community alone. Research in public and external affairs consistently identifies community relations as a part of that function, but does not go into any greater depth.

Methodology

Research Questions
Existing theories provide pieces of the puzzle, but do not fully explain current trends identified in corporate community involvement. The new empirical research undertaken in this study investigates associated gaps (G) in theory and practice by asking the following research questions (RQ):

> G1: *It is not clear whether actions toward the community, considered as a stakeholder group, are motivated by moral factors, economic factors, or some combination of the two.*
>
> RQ1: *What are the drivers behind the concepts of "community as stakeholder" and "community stakeholder management"?*
>
> G2: *There is no theoretical framework to explain how managers define multiple "communities."*
>
> RQ2: *What does "community as stakeholder" mean as an operational concept for company executives and managers?*
>
> G3: *There are no data on the set of managerial actions being taken to address multiple "communities."*
>
> RQ3: (a) *What is the relationship between "community stakeholder management" and the meaning an executive/manager ascribes to "community as stakeholder"? (b) What is the range of actions included within "community stakeholder management"?*

The method chosen to address the three research questions was an extension of grounded theory-building called theory "elaboration" (Strauss, 1987; Strauss and Corbin, 1990, 1994; Vaughan, 1992). This research method employs classic grounded theory techniques (such as constant comparison and theoretical saturation) to extend existing theory by gathering new empirical data. Unlike traditional grounded theory, however, the method assumes that theoretical frameworks exist and can be applied. In this study, therefore, frameworks from stakeholder research, CSR, and sociology are applied, even though theory/practice gaps were identified.

Sample

The firms chosen for the study differed on the basis of two variables: type of industry and corporate social performance (CSP). Twelve companies in the petroleum and retail industries participated in the study. The two industries, chosen for rich comparative analysis, display both similar and dissimilar features. Similar features include a diversity of locations, from big cities to small towns; companies with long histories of community and philanthropic support; and significant external competitive pressures.

The key dissimilar feature between the petroleum and retail industries is the depth of their environmental exposure. The petroleum industry is "dirty," while the retail industry is "clean," from an environmental standpoint. This is an important distinction given the role that environmental issues have played in corporate/community interactions in the past decade.

The Kinder, Lydenberg and Domini (KLD) database, which has received support in the academic community for accurately measuring CSP (Graves and Waddock, 1994; Waddock and Graves, 1997), offers ratings for social screens (Paul and Lydenberg, 1991). Since it does not rank order firms, Waddock and Graves' (1997) KLD ranking scheme was used to develop a composite measure of company social performance related to employees, product, community, the environment, and diversity.

Twelve Fortune 500 corporations (domestic operations only) constituted the sample. This number is large enough for generalizations and rich comparative analysis, yet not too large that data gathering and analysis are overwhelming (Eisenhardt, 1989, 1991). According to an established grounded theory standard, theoretical saturation, the number should be large enough that key themes recur and no new findings are obtained as more sites are added (Glaser and Strauss, 1967; Huberman and Miles, 1994; Post and Andrews, 1982).

Data Collection and Analysis

The key data source was intensive one-hour interviews with managers and executives in a sample of firms. The pilot-tested, standard interview guide followed a semi-structured format, intended to achieve interview consistency, while also allowing interviewees to offer additional relevant information

(Lofland, 1971). Staff, line managers, and executives were interviewed, and interviews were taped, transcribed, and entered into a database to increase the reliability of the qualitative research (Richards and Richards, 1994).

Information was gathered from multiple sources to supplement interviews, such as multiple contacts within each company, supplemented by internal company information and information in the public domain (e.g., annual reports). Use of multiple data sources is encouraged in qualitative research to increase research standards (Gummesson, 1991; Kidder and Judd, 1986; Kirk and Miller, 1986). The intended goal of using multiple data sources here was triangulation of results (Jick, 1979). A data inventory was developed prior to data collection to ensure like and comprehensive data collection from all sites.

Data analysis followed the constant comparative method, another established protocol for qualitative grounded theory research: as information was collected from each firm, it was analyzed in an iterative fashion to heighten understanding of concepts and relationships through the course of the research (Eisenhardt, 1989; Glaser and Strauss, 1967; Strauss and Corbin, 1990; Post and Andrews, 1982; Yin, 1989).

Findings

Drivers for Community Stakeholder Management

Managers and executives clearly articulated three categories of motivating forces for corporate community involvement:

1. *An economic rationale*: the activity was necessitated by strategic goals.
2. *A moral rationale*: corporate values determined support of a certain local activity.
3. *A combined values/strategy approach*: pre-existing corporate values are merged with new corporate strategic realities.

Half of the firms in the sample indicated that the combined economic/moral model is driving their decision-making. Petroleum firms showed a higher tendency than retail firms to make decisions based on strategic rationales.

Of the six firms identifying a combination approach, five identified it as a shift in the past five years. Prior to that, decisions were made more on a values/moral basis. This level of change activity was a significant finding of the research. The shift toward a more economics-driven model was uniform among the retail firms in the combination category. Analysis of the data for corporate social performance (CSP) showed that companies with higher CSP tend to display either a strategy-based or combined values/strategy-based approach.

Definitions of Community as Stakeholder

The executives and managers interviewed in this study articulated a sophisticated understanding about the lack of homogeneity among the citizens or groups in the local towns or cities where they have operations. They do not assume that different communities hold similar views, nor do they assume that within each community type there is uniformity of opinion. Their definitions of community, community groups or individual citizens, to which they felt some responsibility, sorted into philosophical and operational categories.

The managers and executives within each of the twelve firms in the sample held a remarkably similar overarching community stakeholder philosophy. A common theme among all those interviewed was that the corporation has some role in all of the cities, towns, neighborhoods, or communities (all these terms were used equally) where it has a presence. More specifically, three common philosophies were discussed by interviewees. The corporation has responsibility:

1. To improve the quality of life in its cities and towns for its employees.
2. Only for the immediate area around its field of operation, and, potentially, for the groups or individuals that could be harmed by its operations.
3. To support local groups whose goals match the firm's interests.

A smaller number of interviewees articulated a stakeholder philosophy encompassing society at large, most often referred to as "the nation." Corporations with large foundations or corporate giving programs discussed this level of responsibility most often. In these organizations, the corporation was considered to have a role in improving general health and welfare, or in acting on certain issues of grave importance to the country (e.g., education reform and drug abuse).

In terms of operational categories of "community," managers consistently talked about "recognized" groups: those with whom the corporation chooses to have a relationship in each locale, either for mutual benefit or because the group could have a negative effect on the corporation. Common examples given were civic groups (e.g., rotary clubs, city and town boards), local regulatory agencies, and a selected group of non-profit, grassroots activist, and environmental organizations. This finding illuminated the greatest disparity between interview information and public domain information. The interviews identified groups that could have negative consequences for the corporation, and a need to proactively seek good relations with these groups. The public domain information, however, placed emphasis on groups with which the organization holds mutual interests, using labels such as "community partners."

"Ignored" groups make up a second category of operational community. Identified in this group were non-profit organizations and citizen groups having interests not shared by the corporation. Some executives mentioned that these groups are monitored on an ongoing basis, in case they should move into the "recognized" category.

Those individuals the corporation chooses to recognize make up the final community stakeholder category. Cited in this category were employees, customers, potential customers, and local officials (e.g., mayors).

Community Stakeholder Management

Data on corporate actions taken toward the "recognized" individuals and groups above could be sorted into "relationship" and "programmatic" categories. Relationship management activities were uniform across organizations: volunteerism to local non-profit organizations; service by executives on non-profit boards; proactive meetings with city and regulatory officials; and proactive communication with grassroots and environmental groups. Relationship management activities differed by industry: retail companies make a big effort to interact proactively with local officials, especially when attempting to place a new store in a locale; petroleum companies are more likely to spend energy on building good relations with environmental groups and local regulatory officials, given their higher exposure on environmental issues.

The programmatic component of community stakeholder management included a range of activities. The most common was monetary contribution, followed by volunteerism, mentoring, support of local community functions, and crisis outreach. Corporate respondents noted a significant increase in both the number and type of volunteer programs in recent years. Retail and petroleum companies did not differ significantly in the types of programs they offered. The specific emphases or recipients of the contributions and volunteer programs did differ, with managers clearly naming two determining factors: a link to strategy and a link to local circumstances. Petroleum companies support higher education, particularly science and technology programs, because of their need for highly skilled workers and new technology. Retail firms support family and child-oriented non-profit initiatives, because their customer base is most interested in these issues.

Both organizational structure and administrative responsibility for community stakeholder management were explored in the course of the study. A majority of the managers and executives interviewed believed that relationship activities were a shared responsibility among all executives and managers in the organization. While they do look to community relations staff for assistance and training, local line managers handle the interface with community organizations. For programmatic responsibilities, local managers noted that they rely heavily on community relations staff for administrative guidance and ideas, even though they have significant input into programmatic decisions. Several community relations managers identified this struggle between centralization and decentralization. Decisions about local organizations that will receive support (money and/or labor), are being shifted down to the local level.

Analysis of the data for community stakeholder management showed two features that distinguished between firms with high and low corporate social performance. First was the intensity with which the firms managed the relationship and programmatic components of their corporate/community links. Corporations with higher CSP offer more programs, have more volunteers, more groups in their "recognized" categories, and take more time to monitor the local groups contained within the "ignored" category than lower CSP firms. Secondly, firms with high CSP include line employees, and include them in higher numbers, in the decision-making process for community involvement than lower CSP firms.

Theoretical and Practical Implications

This study provides empirical data suggesting that a re-evaluation is needed of stakeholder and CSR frameworks which assert that responsibility to the community as stakeholder is predominantly driven by morals or values. The argument was made that the normative or morally based portions of stakeholder literature include community groups because economic stakeholder frameworks do not cover these interests. In the CSR literature, a similar stream of research labels community and philanthropic work as discretionary, but economic responsibilities as fundamental to company operations. In the sample of companies included in this study, community involvement is clearly motivated by economic drivers. The study confirms and further elaborates the theory/practice gap. In theoretical terms, this finding moves community stakeholder activities from Mitchell, Agle, and Wood's (1997) second "narrow" stakeholder category–stakeholder as moral interest–into their first "narrow" definition–stakeholder as economic interest. Using Carroll's (1979) pyramid model in the CSR literature, present findings move philanthropic and community activities lower down the pyramid, toward its economic base.

The combined strategy/values category found in this study shows that moral bases are still at work, but that increased action is associated with more recent economic/strategic drivers. This category provides another framework–similar to Useem's research on philanthropy and Miles' work in external affairs–that presents corporate social action as being driven by a complex interplay of economic and moral forces, not by simply one or the other.

The findings from this research provide a strong basis for elaborating community stakeholder definitions. The background discussion pointed out

Barbara W. Altman

that practicing managers in our diverse and global environment cannot assume the community homogeneity that currently exists in the literature. The study's findings confirm that managers are well aware that they must tailor community stakeholder definitions to local conditions. The contingency theory applications identified as promising in the CSR literature (Miles, 1987) are indeed applicable in the current community context. This study brings the contingency framework into the stakeholder realm. The findings for community groups and individuals to which the corporation is responsive can be summarized as a new contribution to stakeholder theory:

> "Community as stakeholder" can be defined as those groups or individuals having mutual interests with the firm, those located within the immediate vicinity of the firm's operations, and those having the power to negatively impact the corporation's operations. Corporate actors in individual corporations at single locales where a company has operations determine the identification of stakeholders.

Building further on this framework, three operational definitions of community stakeholders are:

1. Groups "recognized" by the firm;
2. Individuals "recognized" by the firm; and
3. Groups "ignored" by the firm.

The new definition and operational categories of community stakeholder groups confirm Mitchell, Agle, and Wood's (1997) "theory of salience." The study shows that managers are making decisions on the relative importance of stakeholder groups based on factors such as power. Further elaborating Mitchell, Agle, and Wood's (1997) framework, is the finding that an active management function in high CSP firms is the monitoring of "ignored" groups to see if these groups should be moved into a "recognized" category.

The study's findings bring a basic tenet of stakeholder theory into the community context; that is, there is a close association between definitions of stakeholder groups and the managerial actions taken toward those groups. A definition of community stakeholder management follows from the new definition of community as stakeholder:

> "Community stakeholder management" is the set of relationship and programmatic actions that corporate actors choose to engage in, based on the groups or individuals having mutual interests with the firm, those located within the immediate vicinity of the firm's operations, and those having the power to negatively impact the corporation's operations.

This relationship/programmatic framework represents one of the first attempts to specify a managerial practice theory to understand and design corporate community involvement actions. As the background discussion pointed out, previous research in neither philanthropy nor public affairs has offered much insight for community relations executives or line managers interacting at the local level. The finding that high corporate social performance was distinguished by increased levels of relationship and programmatic action provides a goal for companies striving to improve.

The struggle in sociology to refine definitions of *gemeinschaft* and *gesellschaft* was identified earlier as another promising framework for definitions of community as stakeholder. The definition derived in this study achieves one of sociology's goals: it acknowledges the diversity of groups and individuals within a community. Even so, the corporate context is somewhat different than what sociologists might seek, since power and economic dynamics can prevent all opinions from being considered, as the finding of an "ignored" group shows.

The study began with the goal of moving corporate community affairs beyond something that was "bewilderingly complex" for managers to practice (Mitchell, Agle, and Wood, 1997: 857). The definitions derived offer insights to practicing managers into the struggles they face in determining appropriate corporate action toward their multiple "communities." The contingency definition offers a new framework to make sense of corporate community involvement in our diverse society, where no assumptions of homogeneity can be made. The categorization of groups to which corporations are responsible under the community umbrella gives executives and managers guidance on how they can make difficult decisions about "recognized" community groups. Managers at the local level must be trained in stakeholder concepts so that they can identify the groups within their immediate vicinity whose interests are shared by the firm, and those who can negatively impact the firm's operations. They can then work with community relations staff to design appropriate programs and understand the individuals and groups with which they should establish relationships. Better understanding of community stakeholder management will also enable corporate managers to incorporate employee input for improved community relations, and to monitor the full range of community groups at the local level.

Barbara W. Altman (*altman@unt.edu*) is a lecturer at the University of North Texas, Department of Management (Business Administration Building 315, P.O. Box 305429, Denton, TX 76203-5429) and a Senior Research Associate at the Center for Corporate Community Relations (CCR) at Boston College (*www.bc.edu/cccr*). This report is an extension of her dissertation research, available as *Transforming Corporate Community Relations* (1998) through CCR.

Barbara completed work for her DBA degree with James E. Post at the Boston University School of Management.

---

1   A number of terms are used interchangeably in the literature to describe the range of activities under study here. The most common terms are community relations, community involvement, community affairs, and corporate citizenship. Community relations also refers to the corporate function most typically associated with administering community programs; in this report, community relations will be reserved for that corporate function. Corporate citizenship is a new term being used in the corporate sector to describe community activities; in this report, this term is used only for those studies that specifically say corporate citizenship. The labels "community affairs" and "community involvement" will be used synonymously in the main body of this report to refer to the set of activities relating to local communities in which corporations engage.

References

Alperson, M. 1995. *Giving strategies that add business value.* Report no. 1126. New York: The Conference Board.

Altman, B.W. 1996. Strategic corporate community relations: The results of an exploratory study and future research. In *Proceedings of the Seventh Annual Meeting of the International Association for Business and Society held in Santa Fe, NM, 21-24 March 1996,* ed. J.M. Logsdon and K. Rehbein: 525-529.

Burke, E.M. 1999. *Corporate community relations: The principle of the neighbor of choice.* Westport, CN: Praeger.

Burke, L., Logsdon, J.M., Mitchell, W., Reiner, M., and Vogel, D. 1986. Corporate community involvement in the San Francisco Bay Area. *California Management Review,* 28 (3): 122-141.

Burton, B.K., and Dunn, C.P. 1996. Stakeholder theory and community groups: A new view. In *Proceedings of the Seventh Annual Meeting of the International Association for Business and Society held in Santa Fe, NM, 21-24 March 1996,* ed. J.M. Logsdon and K. Rehbein: 549-554.

Carroll, A.B. 1979. A three-dimensional conceptual model of corporate social performance. *Academy of Management Review,* 4 (4): 497-505.

Carroll, A.B. 1991. The pyramid of corporate social responsibility: Toward the moral management of organizational stakeholders. *Business Horizons,* 34 (July-Aug.): 39-48.

Chandler, A. 1962. *Strategy and structure.* Cambridge, MA: MIT Press.

Clarkson, M.B.E. 1994. A risk-based model of stakeholder theory. In *Proceedings of the Second Toronto Conference on Stakeholder Theory:* [5-15]. Toronto: The Centre for Corporate Social Performance & Ethics, Faculty of Management, University of Toronto.

Clarkson, M.B.E. 1998. Introduction. In *The Corporation and its stakeholders: Classic and contemporary readings,* ed. M.B.E. Clarkson: 1-12. Toronto: University of Toronto Press.

Donaldson, T., and Preston, L.E. 1995. The stakeholder theory of the corporation: Concepts, evidence, and implications. *Academy of Management Review,* 20 (1): 65-91.

Eisenhardt, K.M. 1989. Building theories from case study research. *Academy of Management Review*, 14 (4): 532-550.

Eisenhardt, K.M. 1991. Better stories and better constructs: The case for rigor and comparative logic. *Academy of Management Review*, 16 (3): 620-627.

Etzioni, A. 1992. *The spirit of community: Rights, responsibilities, and the communitarian agenda.* New York: Crown.

Fombrun, C.J. 1996. *Reputation: Realizing value from the corporate image.* Boston, MA: Harvard Business School Press.

Freeman, R.E. 1984. *Strategic management: A stakeholder approach.* Boston: Pitman.

Freeman, R.E.1998. A stakeholder theory of the modern corporation. In *The Corporation and its stakeholders: Classic and contemporary readings*, ed. M.B.E. Clarkson: 125-138. Toronto: University of Toronto Press.

Galasiewicz, J. 1985. *Social organization of an urban grants economy: Corporate contributions to nonprofit organizations.* Orlando, FL: Academic Press.

Galasiewicz, J., and Burt, R.S. 1991. Interorganizational contagion in corporate philanthropy. *Administrative Science Quarterly*, 36 (1) (Mar.): 88-105.

Gardner, J.W. 1991. *Building community.* Washington, DC: Independent Sector.

Garone, S.J., ed. 1995. *Strategic opportunities in corporate community activity.* Report no. 1144. New York: The Conference Board.

Glaser, B.G., and Strauss, A.L. 1967. *The discovery of grounded theory: Strategies for qualitative research.* New York: Aldine deGruyter.

Graves, S.B., and Waddock, S.A. 1994. Institutional owners and corporate social performance. *Academy of Management Journal*, 37 (4): 1043-1046.

Gummesson, E. 1991. *Qualitative methods in management research.* Newbury Park, CA: Sage.

Hanson, K.O. 1994. *Corporate community involvement in Silicon Valley.* Palo Alto, CA: Stanford University.

Heald, M. 1988. *The social responsibilities of business: Company and community, 1900-1960.* New Brunswick, NJ: Transaction Press.

Huberman, A.M., and Miles, M.B. 1994. Data management and analysis methods. In *Handbook of qualitative research*, ed. N.K. Denzin and Y.S. Lincoln: 428-444. Thousand Oaks, CA: Sage.

Jick, T.J. 1979. Mixing qualitative and quantitative methods: Triangulation in action. In *Qualitative Methodology*, ed. J. Van Maanen: 135-148. Newbury Park, CA: Sage.

Kidder, L.H., and Judd, C.M. 1986. *Research methods in social relations.* Fort Worth, TX: Holt, Rinehart, and Winston.

Kirk, J., and Miller, M. 1986. *Reliability and validity in qualitative research.* Beverly Hills, CA: Sage.

Lawrence, P.R., and Lorsch, J.W. 1967. *Organization and environment: Managing differentiation and integration.* Boston: Division of Research, Graduate School of Business Administration, Harvard University.

Litchfield, L. 1997. *Profile of the community relations profession.* Chestnut Hill, MA: The Center for Corporate Community Relations at Boston College.

Lofland, J. 1971. *Analyzing social settings: A guide to qualitative observation and analysis.* Belmont, CA: Wadsworth Publishing.

Barbara W. Altman

Mitchell, R.K., Agle, B.R., and Wood, D.J. 1997. Toward a theory of stakeholder identification and salience: Defining the principle of who and what really counts. *Academy of Management Review*, 22 (4): 853-886.

Miles, R.H. 1987. *Managing the corporate social environment: A grounded theory*. Englewood Cliffs, NJ: Prentice-Hall.

Paul, K., and Lydenberg, S. 1991. Corporate social monitoring: Types, methods, goals. In *Contemporary issues in business and society in the United States and abroad*, ed. K. Paul: 129-154. Lewiston: Edwin Mellon Press.

Post, J.E. 1978. *Corporate behavior and social control*. Reston, VA: Reston Publishing.

Post, J.E., and Andrews, P.N. 1982. Case research in corporation and society studies. *Research in Corporate Social Performance and Policy*, 2: 1-33.

Post, J.E., and Griffin, J.J. 1997. *The state of corporate public affairs: 1996 survey results*. Washington, DC: Foundation for Public Affairs, and Boston, MA: Boston University School of Management, Public Affairs Research Group.

Richards, T.J., and Richards, L. 1994. Using computers in qualitative research. In *Handbook of qualitative research*, ed. N.K. Denzin and Y.S. Lincoln: 445-462. Thousand Oaks, CA: Sage.

Selznick, P. 1992. *The moral commonwealth: Social theory and the promise of community*. Berkeley, CA: University of California Press.

Sharfman, M. 1994. Changing institutional rules: The evolution of corporate philanthropy, 1883-1953. *Business & Society*, 33 (3): 236-269.

Siegfried, J.J., McElroy, K.M., and Biernot-Fawkes, D. 1983. The management of corporate contributions. *Research in Corporate Social Performance and Policy*, 5: 87-102.

Smith, C. 1994. The new corporate philanthropy. *Harvard Business Review*, 72 (3): 105-116.

Strauss, A. 1987. *Qualitative analysis for social scientists*. New York: Cambridge University Press.

Strauss, A., and Corbin, J. 1990. *Basics of qualitative research*. Newbury Park, CA: Sage.

Strauss, A., and Corbin, J. 1994. Grounded theory methodology: An overview. In *Handbook of qualitative research*, ed. N.K. Denzin and Y.S. Lincoln: 273-285. Thousand Oaks, CA: Sage.

Tichy, N.M., McGill, A.R., and St. Clair, L., eds. 1997. *Global corporate citizenship: Doing business in the public eye*. San Francisco, CA: New Lexington Press.

Useem, M. 1988. Market and institutional factors in corporate contributions. *California Management Review*, 30 (2): 77-88.

Useem, M. 1991. Organizational and managerial factors in the shaping of corporate social and political action. *Research in Corporate Social Performance and Policy*, 12: 63-92.

Vaughan, D. 1992. Theory elaboration: The heuristics of case analysis. In *What is a case?*, ed. J. Becker and C. Ragin: 173-202. New York: Cambridge University Press.

Vidaver-Cohen, D. 1996. A stewardship model of business-community relations: Implications for theory and practice. In *Proceedings of the Seventh Annual Meeting of the International Association for Business and Society held in Santa Fe, NM, 21-24 March 1996*, ed. J.M. Logsdon and K. Rehbein: 561-566.

Waddock, S.A., and Boyle, M.E. 1995. The dynamics of change in corporate community relations. *California Management Review*, 37 (4): 125-140.

Waddock, S.A., and Graves, S.B. 1997. The corporate social performance-financial performance link. *Strategic Management Journal*, 18 (4): 303-319.

Yin, R.K. 1989. *Case study research*. Newbury Park, CA: Sage.

Barbara W. Altman

Site Location Practices of Asian Manufacturing Transplants in the United States: Lessons for Stakeholder Management

Brian Shaffer, University of Maryland
Joshua Saunders, University of Maryland

Introduction

Japanese automobile manufacturing in the United States has increased rapidly over the last decade and a half. By 1997, Japanese "transplant" auto manufacturers produced over 2.3 million cars and trucks (Figure 1), or roughly 15 percent of total automobile production in the United States. In 1996, these Japanese firms employed over 40,000 manufacturing workers (Figure 2) and over 300,000 distribution and dealership personnel. Japanese plants purchased over 23 billion dollars in materials from United States-based suppliers, satisfying 64 percent of their sourcing needs domestically.

With the exception of the Toyota-GM joint venture in California, all of these auto-making transplants are clustered in the midwestern United States, and are connected to their suppliers by a network of shared interstate highways converging in Indiana, Ohio, and Kentucky (Kenney and Florida, 1992). While clustered on a large scale, each plant is in a different state, and is separated from any other by about two hundred miles. Though there is regional integration with respect to suppliers, the plants operate independently with respect to employment and community even though they seem to follow very similar location and entry strategies (particularly the three largest, Honda, Toyota, and Nissan). Thus, we do not see the close interdependence of firms found in places such as Silicon Valley, Wall Street, or the Big Three auto firms in Detroit.

In our research, which began as a review of the evolution of Japanese automobile manufacturing in the United States, we interpreted a company's choice of site location as a stakeholder management decision. Although favorable tax incentives and supply chain efficiencies are critical "traditional" factors in siting a plant, their availability in many locations meant that they were not the sole factors for decision-making. Similarly, choosing a location to avoid unions, another commonly offered explanation for siting decisions, seemed too simple, since these firms apparently sought a social climate compatible with a production imperative: hard working, cooperative employees, and minimal distraction from operations focused on productivity and quality. While their motivation in choosing a site might be production efficiency, the Japanese manufacturers have been deliberate and largely successful in the development of their American business practices relating to the social environment.

This paper reviews and interprets scholarly articles, trade press, media reporting, and other publicly available documents to assess factors influencing Japanese firms' site location decisions for their United States-based manufacturing facilities.[1] Since most of the Japanese firms discussed have produced results that make the process look deceptively simple, we briefly examine the case of Hyundai Electronics in Oregon whose start-up has been difficult, despite its apparently similar analysis of site location factors.

Research Sources

The transplants' business practices relating to workplace climate and supplier networks are the subject of much informative scholarship.[2] The sources for the research were primarily documents in the public domain, which included scholarly journals, trade publications, and newspapers. In addition, personal experience provided important insights from the "outside" and "inside" of a firm, since the lead author resided near the Toyota plant in Kentucky for several years and worked with Toyota employees and suppliers.

Site Location Criteria

Because of the mission of the transplants, which is strictly the production of automobiles, their relevant stakeholders form a somewhat shorter list than usual. For example, investors are excluded, since the corporate treasury in Japan provides capital. Similarly, customers are excluded, because the manufacturing operations simply transfer their cars to their companies' sales divisions and have no role in marketing and dealer relations. Key stakeholders considered in this study, then, include employees, suppliers, communities, and state and local governments. It is an important point that nearly all of the key stakeholders are determined and defined by the site location decision.

The relationship with state and local governments and communities is an important and complex consideration for transplant firms: the competition of localities for "the prize" of a major manufacturing plant necessarily affects the transplants' location decisions, but the incentives offered are not sufficient to make the siting decision. Schmenner (1980), in an empirical study

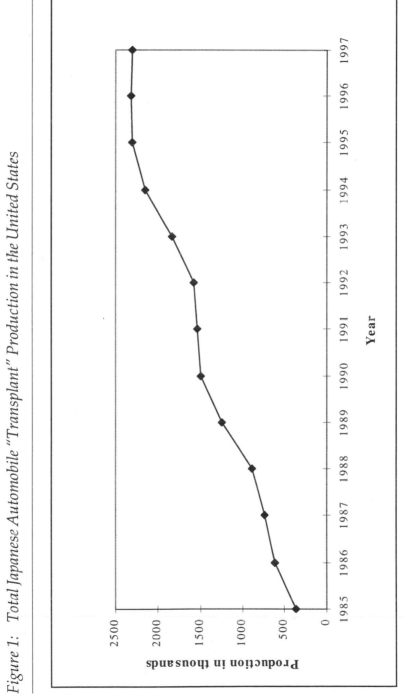

Figure 1: Total Japanese Automobile "Transplant" Production in the United States

(Source: Japanese Automobile Manufacturers Association, 1998.)

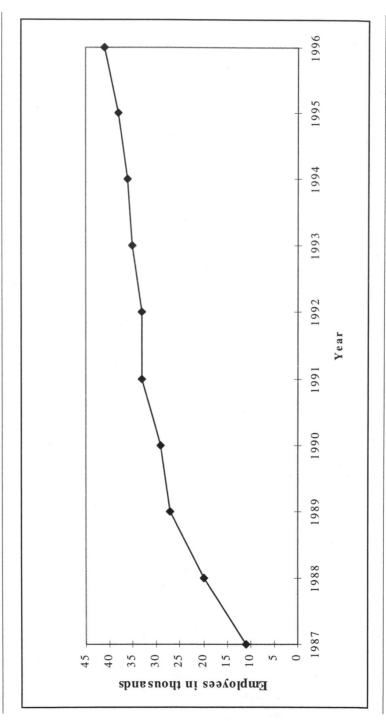

Figure 2: Americans Employed by Japanese Automobile "Transplants" in the United States

(Source: Japanese Automobile Manufacturers Association, 1998.)

Brian Shaffer and Joshua Saunders

of plant location patterns, emphasizes the importance of technical and structural criteria, including wages, union avoidance, access to raw materials, cost of living, population, and education. We suggest that the social environment plays a role that is less visible but equally important. If, for example, enough members of the local community, government, and media contest a firm's plans and operations, the business may survive but perform sub-optimally, thereby over-riding any benefits sought with the initial choice of location.

The American social climate is currently more friendly toward transplants, although their entry to the United States began in the 1980s when the climate was hostile toward Japanese producers. This hostility may have been the result of trade tensions, declining fortunes of the American manufacturing sector, and lingering anti-Japanese sentiments stemming from World War II. Given this history, the transplants realize that they can ill-afford to ignore their stakeholders, and make special efforts to address their reputation in American society. As a result, the Japanese are careful to choose communities where, in addition to economic incentives provided by government, they can secure a favorable climate for business (i.e., cultural stability, a strong work ethic, etc.). They appear to have a strong norm around community-business partnerships (and on choosing locations supportive of this norm).

Most of the plants ultimately located in "greenfield sites," meaning locations that had no previous manufacturing presence or infrastructure (Kenney and Florida, 1992). Because Honda, Toyota, and Nissan each built large plants that dominated small, rural towns, the "greenfield" metaphor also applies to the socio-economic and cultural situation of the host communities they entered.

The transplants enjoyed something that many established firms could not: they were, in effect, able to "choose" their stakeholders by examining the economic and social characteristics of various locales and work forces. The Japanese managers clearly chose sites that replicated aspects of their home country culture. In particular, somewhat isolated communities with homogeneous populations (Table 1) and cultural norms were seen as essential for providing workers capable of cooperative, team-oriented behavior. Social tensions were viewed as a threat to productivity and team unity. Also, pre-employment screening for assembly line jobs in these firms considered not only job skills, education, and health, but also personal values, attitudes, and people skills. These assessments are unusual, when compared to the typical American firm, for such relatively unskilled jobs. Previous experience in auto manufacturing was not an advantage under this system, and few unemployed autoworkers from American firms were hired. The transplant firms could be selective about location and employee traits because they had and have a reputation for offering desirable places to work.

For example, employee and supplier training and quality improvement are extensive; pay, benefits, and job security are excellent; and support for community infrastructure and cultural amenities is always in excess of basic tax and regulatory obligations. These firms are respected and valued in their towns and regions, although they are not entirely without controversy. Significant controversy faced by the transplants has involved labor relations (though none of them are currently unionized), and a sexual harassment scandal at Mitsubishi's Illinois plant. Even so, little sustained record of hostile protesters or critics exists, with the exception of organized labor, a constituency with understandable motives but limited "grassroots" support in most transplant communities.

There are two common criticisms of the transplants' social performance, and these have become less significant as the plants mature. First, some critics point to the strain that demanding standards of quality and productivity place on workers and suppliers. Clearly, the standards are tougher than those found in unionized plants, and some workers are fired for inadequate performance. However, complaints about the demands of the assembly line and the practice of compulsory overtime are common to many manufacturing settings, including those with unionized labor. Second, due to the location of the plants, there are very few employees from minority groups (Cole and Deskins, 1988). The firms claim, correctly, that they employ minorities in excess of their representation in the local population, but most operate in largely white communities. Their critics believe that the site location choices were motivated partly by an effort to avoid minority populations. While Japanese managers talk about homogeneity and social unity, their critics see deliberate exclusion.

In summary, the Japanese transplants have relied on carefully executed strategies to develop and manage their stakeholder relationships. Based on the sources reviewed, and on the firms' growth patterns, these firms appear successful in calming the protectionist sentiments of Americans and also in cultivating productive and loyal suppliers and employees.

Hyundai in Eugene, Oregon[3]

Given our emphasis on diligence in the site location decisions of Toyota, Honda, and other Japanese transplants, it is interesting to look for parallels in other Asian manufacturing transplants. In 1995, Hyundai Corporation announced it would invest $1.3 billion in a semiconductor fabrication plant in Eugene, Lane County, Oregon. Employment was projected at 800 jobs, a level that had indeed been attained by 1999. This plant was not only Hyundai's first outside Korea, but also the first built in the United States by a Korean company.

Hyundai's home country, industry, and site location choice were different from the Japanese automobile manufacturers, but there were also numer-

Brian Shaffer and Joshua Saunders

Table 1: Demographics of Japanese Automobile Manufacturing Sites in the United States (1990 Census Data)

County, State	Manufacturer	Population	Per Capita Income ($US)	High School Graduation or Higher (%)	BA or Higher (%)	Born in State of Residence (%)	Foreign-Born (%)	White (%)	Black (%)	Asian (%)	Hispanic (%)
Scott, KY	Toyota	23,867	12,314	69.1	15.2	79.9	0.0	93.0	6.3	0.8	0.3
Union, OH	Honda	31,969	13,644	76.2	12.0	84.2	0.1	95.6	3.7	0.4	0.2
Rutherford, TN	Nissan	118,570	12,536	73.9	18.7	66.1	1.8	89.2	9.0	1.4	0.2
McLean, IL	Mitsubishi	129,180	14,138	84.7	29.0	77.9	1.9	93.7	4.3	1.3	1.3
Tippecano, IN	Subaru-Isuzu	130,598	12,570	85.2	30.7	69.0	5.1	93.4	2.0	3.7	1.6
United States	(average)	248,709,873	14,420	76.8	20.3	67.1	7.7	80.3	12.1	2.9	9.0

(Source: U.S. Census Bureau, 1999.)

ous similarities in the decision-making process. Hyundai also used a greenfield plant model, and chose Eugene freely from among many attractive locations. In support of their choice, Hyundai managers cited a combination of governmental incentives, proximity to suppliers and customers, and the availability of knowledge workers. Lane County, Oregon, is racially homogenous, but also contains an important state university which generates more social and political diversity than the broader demographics might suggest.

Hyundai announced that the building of the Oregon plant was the first part of a three-phase expansion in the United States, including future expansion in Eugene. Hyundai's North American CEO stated that Oregon was chosen "because it is close to customers and because it is a gateway where many future technologies are evolving . . . [and because of] its ease of access to transportation, its strong resource base and its proximity to our future business on the Pacific Rim" (Anonymous, 1995). In the end, Eugene was chosen over Fort Collins, Colorado, and a Dallas suburb. The location of other microchip plants in Oregon partially contributed to the decision: Intel and Fujitsu both had large design and production facilities in and around the Portland area. Taxes also played a role in the decision, since Hyundai was exempt, under the enterprise zone program, from paying property taxes for the first three years of the Eugene plant's existence. The *New York Times* summarized that "Eugene prevailed by virtue of its plentiful water supply, inexpensive energy, an abundant skilled work force, attractive quality of life and–not coincidentally–tax breaks" (Zimmerman, 1995: D3).

Controversy
Despite the increase in jobs for the region, not everyone welcomed Hyundai with open arms. At a town meeting soon after the announcement, opponents in Eugene seized on the issues of wetland destruction and the flow of unchecked hazardous waste. In response, the executive director of the Eugene-Springfield Partnership, a non-profit organization that promotes development in the area, defended the cleanliness of the chip industry, saying, "This is not ticky-tacky industry. This is clean, light manufacturing in a campus-type setting. There'll always be complaints, but most people are more realistic. There's nothing worse than living in a beautiful area without a job" (Zimmerman, 1995: D3).

Hyundai broke ground on its Eugene chip plant in December 1995. The company initially fulfilled the majority of environmental permit requirements, but refused to draft an environmental impact statement, claiming that it would excessively delay production. Three environmental organizations sought a temporary restraining order to prevent Hyundai from moving ahead with the plant. Although the court denied the petition, it set a hearing date for the issue of a permanent injunction, which was finally denied.

Brian Shaffer and Joshua Saunders

From the beginning, seemingly routine issues such as zoning and property taxes mired the chipmaker's progress. Hyundai made obvious contributions to the local economy and employment, but its plant was located on wetlands, and its manufacturing process involved the transport and use of toxic chemicals. While industrial zoning permits made wetland development legal, and there is no question that Hyundai complied with the law, that did not stop social activists from protesting the company's presence.

Soon after the construction began, Hyundai opponents chained themselves to equipment at the site, resulting in several arrests. The protestors cited multiple issues: "everything from the environmental impact of the facility to the type of employer Hyundai would be to the traffic it would generate" (Williams, 1998). This opposition became so intense that Hyundai cancelled milestone celebrations, fearing that they would be used as platforms for disruption.

Ultimately, due to environmental opposition and judicial reviews of construction permits, the plant opening was delayed by nearly eighteen months, reportedly costing Hyundai $200 million (Anonymous, 1998). Despite the 800 jobs added by 1999, the Korean chipmaker continues to meet opposition. Most recently, a new dimension of social performance has emerged, to the firm's embarrassment: employment discrimination allegations have led to civil fines of $14 million and a formal condemnation from the Eugene Human Rights Commission (Palmer, 1999).

When compared to the experiences of Toyota in Kentucky, and Honda in Ohio, the discrimination problem raises obvious questions about stakeholder management, especially because the demographics in these locations are so similar: Lane County, Oregon, is 95 percent white, and less than 1 percent black. Yet the hostile questioning of Hyundai's hiring practices was characterized as coming from a "vocal minority" within the local community (Baker, 1998). This was certainly not the case for the auto transplants in the midwest (although the latter did face critics outside their local areas).

The question of "where did they go wrong?" is subject to interpretation, but Baker (1998: 17-19) blames both poor implementation and ill-informed site selection. Although he does not consider the question posed in this paper about "choosing stakeholders," specific mistakes identified in evaluating Hyundai's entry in Eugene include:

1. Lack of initial investigation.
2. Gross underestimation of the importance of cultural differences between the host community and Hyundai managers.
3. Failure to involve local community leaders in early stages of development.

The result of these failings is that the plant's adversaries used any possible means to be disruptive, even if that meant holding Hyundai to higher standards than other firms in the area (Baker, 1998: 10).

Assessment

The material described provides the basis for normative comparisons of firm performance on both economic and social dimensions. This experience certainly suggests the importance of stakeholder analysis as a necessary complement to the economic and financial modeling of site location decisions. Baker (1998) uses the metaphor of a "blind date" to describe Hyundai's entry into Eugene, Oregon, which usefully depicts a scenario in which a suitor has evaluated the statistical attributes of a prospective date, but knows nothing about his/her personality.

The evidence gathered hardly suggests that Hyundai's difficulties were the result of pernicious intentions. More likely, the firm used poor planning and poor stakeholder management simply because it failed to anticipate social issues in the community, especially environmental concerns. Toyota and Honda made full use of the greenfield concept by moving to small rural locations that were still within twenty or thirty miles of major research universities. Both categorically avoided social activists with their choice of plant location. By contrast, Hyundai located in a community with a concentration of activists.

Conclusions

Japanese auto transplants in the midwestern United States, as documented by studies cited above, have been successful in terms of both the company (e.g., production and growth), and the community (e.g., spin-off benefits of local economic development and employment). We leave it to the reader to conclude whether siting policies carefully formulated to avoid social tensions are justified in the quest for production efficiency.

The greenfield metaphor implies "new beginnings" and a place where a firm can focus primarily on the profit imperative. In the same vein, we know that individuals abandon their locational roots in search of optimal housing, employment, and schools for their children. Most people would not criticize individuals for making such decisions, even as we observe the negative social consequences. Should we castigate business firms for similar behaviors? If we choose to do so, we should be realistic in accounting for the economic and financial constraints those firms face. At the same time, we can be critical of the trade-offs. Optimal stakeholder management, at least in some circumstances, is indeed constrained by the economic imperative. In that sense, Hyundai could have found a better place to do business.

The initial concerns of the people of Oregon were similar to those faced by Toyota in Kentucky, Honda in Ohio, and Nissan in Tennessee–especially in terms of increased traffic and pollution. Yet the Japanese car makers worked out such problems without serious disruption. The difference is that they were operating within relatively cooperative local community and government environments, and used philanthropic and outreach strategies to maintain good relations. It is our assessment that these Japanese firms demonstrated careful consideration of stakeholders, including potential stakeholders, as a necessary step toward production efficiency.

Brian Shaffer (*Brian_Shaffer@rhsmith.umd.edu*) is Assistant Professor of Business and Public Policy at the Robert H. Smith School of Business, University of Maryland, College Park, MD 20742-1815.

Joshua Saunders is a 1998 MBA Graduate of the Robert II. Smith School of Business, University of Maryland. He is currently a manager with the Washington Post Companies.

[1] Note that this paper looks only at manufacturing facilities. Responsibilities for functions such as design, sales, and distribution are determined in separate corporate divisions, which are not considered here.

[2] There is a considerable literature on the Japanese transplants' business practices (e.g., Besser, 1996; Florida and Kenney, 1991; Perrucci, 1994). This literature is often concerned with organization theory questions such as whether employee and supplier relations systems replicate practices found in Japan (e.g., keiretsu networks and team-based governance of shop operations). There are also scholarly works explicitly critical of Japanese labor relations practices (e.g., Graham, 1993; Rehder, 1990).

[3] The comparison with Hyundai was inspired by Baker (1998). Reporter Lance Robertson of the Eugene Register-Guard helpfully answered questions over the telephone.

References

Anonymous, 1995. Hyundai picks Oregon for chip plant. *United Press International*, May 22.

Anonymous, 1998. Oregon construction delays cost Hyundai $200 million. *Seattle Times*, Feb. 18: C1.

Baker, K.L. 1998. *Facilitating expansion: Hyundai's blind date with an American community*. Corporate Citizenship Research Paper Series. Chestnut Hill, MA: The Center for Corporate Community Relations at Boston College.

Besser, T.L. 1996. *Team Toyota: Transplanting the Toyota culture to the Camry plant in Kentucky*. Albany, NY: State University of New York (SUNY) Press.

Cole, R.E., and Deskins, D.R. 1988. Racial factors in site location and employment patterns of Japanese auto firms in America. *California Management Review*, 31 (1) (Fall): 9-22.

Florida, R., and Kenney, M. 1991. Transplanted organizations: The transfer of Japanese industrial organization to the U.S. *American Sociological Review*, 56 (3) (June): 381-398.

Graham, L. 1993. Inside a Japanese transplant: A critical perspective. *Work and Occupations*, 20 (2) (May): 147-173.

Japanese Automobile Manufacturers Association. 1998. *The motor industry of Japan.* Washington, DC: The Association.

Kenney, M., and Florida, R. 1992. Japanese transplants: Production, organization, and regional development. *Journal of the American Planning Association*, 58 (1) (Winter): 21-38.

Palmer, S. 1999. Hyundai practices in hiring censured. *Eugene Register-Guard*, Sept. 22: C1.

Perrucci, R. 1994. *Japanese auto transplants in the heartland: Corporatism and community.* New York: Aldine De Gruyter.

Rehder, R.R. 1990. Japanese transplants: After the honeymoon. *Business Horizons*, 33 (1) (Jan./Feb.): 87-98.

Schmenner, R.W. 1980. How corporations select communities for new manufacturing plants. In *The economics of firm size, market structure, and social performance*, ed. J.J. Siegfried: 182-201. Washington, DC: U.S. Government Printing Office.

U.S. Census Bureau. 1999. *State & county quick facts*, http://www.census.gov. (Sept.) [Website used to retrieve 1990 census data.]

Williams, E. 1998. Seeing the sun in a storm. *The Oregonian*, http://www.oregonlive.com/todaysnews/9804/st04126.html (Apr. 12).

Zimmerman, R. 1995. Oregon's Silicon Forest lures new factories. *New York Times*, June 26: D3.

Brian Shaffer and Joshua Saunders

Part 3

Outcomes and Evaluation

Managerial Opportunism and Firm Performance: An Empirical Test of Instrumental Stakeholder Theory

Shawn Berman, Boston University

Introduction

Problems associated with the separation of firm ownership and control have been noted by organizational theorists since before Berle and Means (1932). Much of the research in this area, however, has been carried out by agency theorists concerned only with the relationship between managers and stockholders. This research extends the work on the effects of managerial opportunism on corporate performance to include other primary stakeholders. Using data from three key stakeholders in the wood products industry, this study offers two main contributions. First, it represents an important addition to the work in corporate social performance (CSP) by using Data Envelopment Analysis (DEA) to allow for the construction of a true multidimensional measure of corporate performance. Second, it adds to the literature on the link between chief executive officer (CEO) compensation and firm performance.

Background is provided on instrumental stakeholder theory and research linking executive pay to firm performance (the pay-performance link). The methodology and results of the present empirical study are briefly described.

Background

Instrumental Stakeholder Theory

After the publication of Freeman's (1984) seminal work, scholarly interest in stakeholder theory rose dramatically. Donaldson and Preston (1995), in a review article a decade later, identify three streams within stakeholder theory development. Among these is instrumental stakeholder theory (Donaldson and Preston, 1995; Jones, 1995), which provides the theoretical foundation for this study. This theory hypothesizes a connection between an action and an outcome, and makes predictions on the normative assumption that all stakeholders deserve moral consideration. For example, many authors have suggested that trust between managers and key stakeholders can lead to competitive advantage for firms. Jones' (1995) work on instrumental stakeholder theory suggests reasons behind this advantage. That is, fundamentally, a manager who strives to treat all stakeholders fairly will cultivate trust which might manifest itself as a reputation as a preferred trading partner (Shapiro, Sheppard, and Cheraskin, 1992). Firms employing these managers will save money in many areas, including costs associated with problems of agency (Jensen and Meckling, 1976), such as contracting (Barney and Hansen, 1994; Hill, 1995; Jones, 1995; Ring and Van de Ven, 1992), as well as decreased production costs associated with increased flexibility and true "teamwork" among employees. Managers who act opportunistically, however, will be unable to capture these positive benefits, and may preclude some transactions from occurring, because establishing adequate trust levels with important stakeholders will be impossible to achieve. In effect, "a reputation for trustworthiness is really a reputation for not being opportunistic" (Jones, 1995: 421).

Jones' (1995) basic claim is that positive (but, not necessarily financial) benefits will accrue to firms that act in accordance with this belief. However, it is important to note that demonstrating this positive relationship does not elucidate the motivations of those representing the firm, except that individuals would have difficulty "faking" such a moral posture over an extended period (Frank, 1988).

The work in instrumental stakeholder theory begins to provide a framework to advance stakeholder theory in a way that is both empirically tractable and has clear implications for managers. Until now, the array of work under the broad rubric of stakeholder theory, and fundamental disagreement about the theory's basic assumptions, have probably impeded theorists from advancing beyond the foundational precept that "stakeholders matter." Without such consensus, theorists have largely been unable to give more depth to stakeholder theory. Instead, theorists develop and elaborate different "normative cores" (Freeman, 1994): sets of underlying, guiding moral principles that provide a basis for managerial action and corporate governance. Donaldson and Preston (1995) argue that the normative arguments are the most important in establishing the justification of stakeholder theory. However, the lack of regard for its empirical and mainstream social science applications, combined with the inability to reach consensus, probably hamper the acceptance of the theory among the wider body of managerial scholars and practitioners.

Executive Compensation

The link between executive pay and firm performance has been studied for over seventy years (Gomez-Mejia, 1994), with firm performance almost always measured solely in financial terms, particularly shareholder wealth creation. To date, however, no clear, consistent link between executive pay and firm financial performance exists, possibly due to the lack of a solid theoretical basis for expecting such a relationship (Gomez-Mejia, 1994). To explain this relationship, some authors on managerial theory (Aoki, 1984; Davis, 1991; Herman, 1981; Kosnik, 1987; Marris, 1964) suggest that top executives may have the power to influence boards of directors to negotiate salaries unwarranted from an agency or stakeholder theory perspective, given the firm's performance. Others suggest that top managers are compensated for political and ceremonial functions which may not be directly related to firm financial performance (e.g., Cyert and March, 1963; Meyer and Rowan, 1977; Weick, 1979). Still others assert that a strictly linear link between executive pay and financial goals would ignore a top manager's other core responsibilities (Ungson and Steers, 1984). Finally, tournament theory suggests that large compensation packages represent a reward for climbing to the top of the corporation which motivates lower level managers.

Recently, researchers have used agency theory to examine the pay-per-formance link, suggesting that managers should be rewarded for diverting most of the surplus value of the firm to its shareholders. But, the assumption that such a strict tie should exist between shareholder and managerial increases in wealth implies that the effects of managerial actions on other stakeholder groups can be safely ignored. This could have the disquieting side-effect of implicitly rewarding managers to undertake actions which may actually harm other stakeholder groups, so long as shareholder enrichment is the outcome (Freeman, 1994), or rewarding managers for engineering short-term increases in stock price at the expense of long-term performance. If the interests of all stakeholders are taken seriously, then the obsession of agency theorists with strengthening the link between CEO pay and firm financial performance is morally disturbing. Fundamental to stakeholder theory, as used in this study, is that managers are agents for all stakeholders. Therefore, executive compensation should be examined in relation to a measure of performance based on key stakeholder groups, rather than just financial performance.

Further, it is not clear that the connection between compensation and performance should be strictly linear. Executive salaries perceived to be "out of line" by employees and other key stakeholders may erode the basis necessary for trust between management and stakeholders. Indeed, many scholars in both strategic management and ethics have begun to focus on the need for managers to establish cooperative relationships between the firm and its stakeholders (e.g., Barney and Hansen, 1994; Hill, 1990; and Solomon, 1992).

The instrumental stakeholder approach developed by Jones (1995) implies that how managers deal with one stakeholder group represents a signal to other stakeholders to trust managers or be wary of managerial opportunism.

In this study, managerial opportunism is measured as the ability of the CEO to negotiate a pay package far above the industry average. This serves as a signal to stakeholders that the CEO may be interested in short-term gains, without contemplating the long-term prospects for the organization. This may be especially true when large compensation packages are awarded to executives during times of distress within the company (e.g., downsizing, or, more generally, stagnant front line salaries [Sloan, 1996]).

This research, therefore, represents a step toward adding empirical rigor to stakeholder theory, by focusing directly on the consequences of managerial action. While some stakeholder theorists argue for a shift away from managers as a perceived central focus in stakeholder theory (e.g., Calton, 1996; Calton and Kurland, 1996; Calton and Lad, 1995), the current study addresses the dearth of material on the role of managers in stakeholder theory. Jones' (1995) work, on managerial responsibilities beyond an obligation to maximize firm value, is used as a foundation. The study applies instrumental stakeholder theory to executive compensation, suggesting that CEOs whose compensation is far above the industry average will be perceived as diverting organizational resources for their own enrichment. Such opportunistic behavior will be correlated with decreased firm performance, as measured across three "primary" stakeholder groups: shareholders, employees, and community (as represented by effects on the natural environment) (Clarkson, 1995; Evan and Freeman, 1993).

Hypotheses

Two hypotheses are tested using standard regression techniques. First, the arguments articulated in the paragraphs above would suggest:

H1: Firms with excessively high levels of executive compensation, relative to the industry average, will exhibit lower levels of performance.

Compensation packages, while they can differ markedly from firm to firm, have three basic components: salary or base pay, annual bonuses, and long-term incentive pay (Gomez-Mejia, 1994). Empirically, salaries tend to show little variation, after controlling for firm size and industry (Steers and Ungson, 1987). While theoretical reasons for this finding are unclear, boards of directors may set CEO salaries based on those at similar organizations, or public expectations may force salaries into a tight band (Gomez-Mejia, 1994). More variation would be expected in bonuses and long-term incentives, because they are linked directly to firm performance which is variable. These more complicated forms of compensation may also allow opportunistic managers to divert firm resources to their own enrichment with less scrutiny. While some stock option packages have come to the attention of the business press (e.g., Sloan, 1996), these awards are rarely reported outside of proxy filings with the Securities and Exchange Commission (SEC). CEOs may be tempted, therefore, to negotiate lucrative bonus and option plans *in lieu* of high salaries to avoid the criticism of being "over paid." If this were the case, we could expect the following:

> *H2: The negative relationship between excessive compensation and firm performance will strengthen as the form of compensation becomes more complex.*

Research Methods

Sample
This study uses data from a single industry, specifically the wood products industry, to test these hypotheses. Confining the study to a single industry is important, since firms in different industries face different stakeholder issues (see Clarkson, 1995; Griffin and Mahon, 1997). The final sample was forty-four firms from the population of 160 publicly traded firms from the two-digit U.S. Standard Industrial Classification (SIC) codes 24 and 26. Data were collected for three years, from 1993 to 1995, yielding 132 total observations.

Data Analysis
Data analysis was performed in two stages. First, the measure of corporate performance was calculated using Data Envelopment Analysis (DEA). The second phase utilized the Time Series Cross Section (TSCS) function in LIMDEP (Greene, 1992). This function estimates generalized least squares (GLS) regressions by examining the relationship between corporate performance and signs of managerial opportunism.[1] While regression analysis is commonly used in the management literature, the use of DEA is relatively novel outside of operations research and management science. Briefly, DEA is a linear programming technique that allows for a single measure of firm activity to be generated from multiple input and output measures (Howard and Miller, 1993). By estimating a "best practices frontier," DEA shows how efficiently a firm is converting inputs into outputs. Or, in this case, how well the firm is using internal mechanisms to satisfy stakeholder concerns. (For a more thorough review of DEA, see Charnes, *et al.* [1994], and the appendix of Bendheim, Waddock, and Graves [1998: 330-336].) For this study, the inputs for shareholders were CEO/board chairperson duality, classified boards, and the proportion of outside directors, while the output was shareholder return. For effects on the natural environment, Toxics Release Inventory data were used to calculate the firm's commitment to recycling for the input side,

while toxic emissions were used as the output. Finally, employee inputs were the presence of employee stock option plans, and profit sharing arrangements. The output variable was the number of Occupational Safety and Health Administration (OSHA) violations issued against the firm. From this data, firm performance was calculated for each firm-year. This variable is the dependent variable in a regression analysis involving three different models involving different forms of executive compensation.

Independent variables are:

1. *CEO compensation* in a different form for each model, moving from the least to most complex form of compensation.

In model 1, compensation is measured simply as salary (base pay); in model 2, the compensation variable comprises salary and bonuses, as well as other annual compensation and the cash value of perquisites, as reported in proxy statements. Finally, in model 3, the compensation variable includes all of the forms of compensation listed in model 2 and the value of all "in the money" stock options.

2. *Excess compensation*: a dichotomous variable calculated by assessing a CEO's compensation package relative to the industry mean.

This variable was coded "1" if the compensation, adjusted for firm size, was more than 1.5 standard deviations from the mean compensation level. The demarcation of 1.5 standard deviations above the mean was chosen, as such values are relatively rare (or as Tukey, 1977, calls them, "outside the box").

Control variables included in the regressions are:

1. *Firm size*, as measured by the natural log of firm assets, included since larger firms have more resources to distribute among key stakeholders.
2. *Two-digit SIC code*, as a dummy variable, included to accommodate different operating environments in the two segments of the industry (harvesting of trees and the processing of lumber).

Results and Analysis

Table 1 provides the descriptive statistics and correlation coefficients for the continuous variables. The variance inflation factors (VIFs) showed no multicollinearity problems. While collinearity is certainly present, the observed values of the VIFs never exceeded the critical limit of 10 (Neter, Wasserman, and Kutner, 1989).

Table 2 reports the results for the three regressions. Model 3 includes only 40 firms (120 observations) because of incomplete data on options. H1

Table 1: Descriptive Statistics and Correlations

Variable	Mean	s.d.	Performance	LnAssets	Salary/ Sales	Compensation/ Sales	(Compensation+Options)/ Sales
Performance	0.47	0.29	1.0000				
LnAssets	13.96	1.66	0.1906	1.0000			
Salary/Sales	0.60	0.67	-0.0776	-0.6035**	1.0000		
Compensation/Sales	1.28	1.95	-0.0348	-0.4789**	0.8793**	1.0000	
(Compensation+Options)/Sales	2.66	5.23	-0.2081*	-0.3005**	0.8616**	0.8420**	1.0000

*p<.05, **p<.01

Table 2: Regression Analysis

Dependent variable is performance

	Model 1 Salary $n=44$	Model 2 Total Cash Compensation $n=44$	Model 3 Compensation + "In the Money" Options $n=40$
Constant	-0.273	-0.326*	0.008
	(0.273)	(0.149)	(0.137)
SIC	-0.022	-0.044	-0.044
	(0.054)	(0.028)	(0.032)
LnAssets	0.049**	0.051***	0.031**
	(0.018)	(0.011)	(0.010)
Salary/Sales	0.053		
	(0.043)		
Excess Salary	-0.133		
	(0.117)		
Total Comp/Sales		0.050***	
		(0.011)	
Excess Total Comp		-0.150*	
		(0.070)	
Comp+Options/Sales			0.007
			(0.005)
Excess Comp+Options			-0.368**
			(0.127)
G^2	453.12	452.82	405.22

*p<.05, **p<.01, ***p<.001

received support in the analyses using total cash compensation and compensation including the value of "in the money" stock options. The variable representing CEOs with supranormal compensation was negative and significant in both models 2 and 3 (t=2.14, p<.05; t=2.90, p<.01, respectively). The data, therefore, show a negative relationship between firm performance and excessive executive compensation, giving support to instrumental stakeholder theory, as presented here. H2 was also supported: the relationship between performance and excess compensation strengthened as the measure of compensation became more complex. This is supportive of the idea that CEOs primarily interested in personal gain will seek more discreet ways to accrue these gains.

It is interesting to note that in all three models the coefficient on the measure of compensation exhibited a positive relationship to firm performance. It was significant, however, only in model 2 (t=4.55, p<.001). That this variable was highly statistically significant in model 2, and not significant in models 1 or 3, is somewhat perplexing. It may be that salaries are subject to slight variance, while stock options can be de-coupled from performance with more ease than bonuses and other forms of annual compensation.

Additionally, the variable representing firm size was positive and significant in all three models (t=2.72, p<.01; t=4.64, p<.001; t=3.10, p<.01, respectively). This result is open to a variety of interpretations, but it is clear that larger firms tend to have higher levels of performance. The dichotomous variable capturing the sector of the wood products industry in which the firm operates was not significant in any of the models. This finding supports the view that the measures chosen to construct the performance measure were equally valid for each sector of the industry.

Discussion and Implications

The results of the data analysis provided three clear findings:

1. CEOs whose compensation packages are well above the industry average are associated with firms that perform less well, after controlling for firm size.
2. CEO compensation seems to be positively related to firm performance over most of the range of the data, suggesting that pay and performance are generally associated.
3. Larger firms tend to perform better, all else being equal.

The support for H1 and H2 shows that stakeholders should be wary of excessively large executive compensation packages. The data suggest that executives receiving such pay packages are employed at firms that do not perform well in relation to shareholders, employees, and the natural environment. That is, internally, such firms have board structures which do not allow for shareholder input, do not institute "employee friendly" practices, and show a limited commitment to recycling toxic materials used in production processes. Even when such actions are undertaken, the performance ratings of these firms suggest they deliver lower returns to shareholders, have less-safe work environments, and emit more toxic chemicals into the environment than firms with similar internal structures. As researchers on stakeholders and on trust within organization have theorized, high levels of executive compensation may signal to stakeholders that the firm is not adequately concerned with addressing the needs of important stakeholders.

An important facet about this research is that the relationship is examined in such a way that causality cannot be inferred. It may be that higher pay is needed to attract competent executives at poorly performing firms. Two factors undermine such reasoning. The general linear relationship between compensation and performance shown in all three models suggests that, generally, pay increases with performance. Additionally, the fact that the negative relationship between excessive compensation and performance strengthens as the form of compensation becomes less transparent, implies that boards of directors approve these supranormal pay packages in such a way that the average observer will be less likely to take notice of them. Theoretically, taking the helm at a poorly performing company is a riskier proposition than at a more stable firm (Gomez-Mejia, 1994). From this, we might expect CEOs to demand higher base salaries to shield themselves from the risk that accompanies performance-contingent compensation, such as bonuses and stock options. The relationship should therefore weaken as the compensation includes more complex forms. Thus, the evidence presented here thus seems to support the logic of instrumental stakeholder theory rather than the idea that these compensation packages are necessary to lure talented executives to poorly performing firms.

The ramifications of the support for H1 for firm-stakeholder trust levels deserve some mention. Jones (1995) emphasizes that excessive compensation is a sign of lack of managerial trustworthiness. In turn, many theorists (e.g., Barney and Hansen, 1994; Hill, 1990) have suggested that high trust levels lead to competitive advantage. The findings presented here suggest that the ability to establish trust between managers and stakeholders is undermined in two ways at firms where managers receive extremely large compensation packages. Stakeholders may be less willing to show the respect necessary for trust to develop (Lewicki and Bunker, 1996) in an atmosphere where they perceive the CEO to be "feathering his/her own nest." In addition, the empirical results here suggest such firms actually give shareholders lower returns, workers a less-safe work environment, etc. Thus, stakeholders may be less willing to engage in trusting behaviors, both because they feel the CEO is over-compensated, and because they are not treated in a way that encourages loyalty to the organization. Excessive compensation could, therefore, set in motion a downward spiral in organizational performance, such that stakeholders are less willing to engage in trusting behaviors with representatives of firms where managers are perceived to be over-compensated. This, in turn, leads to higher costs, which lower performance. The combination of large compensation packages and lower performance then leads to further degradation of the stakeholder-management relationship. The beginning of this causal chain, however, is impossible to determine by the methodologies employed in this study.

The finding that the linear compensation term is positively related to performance, and statistically significant in regression model 2, is in agreement with some of the work examining the pay-financial performance link. As discussed above, some researchers have found a positive relationship between executive pay and firm financial performance (e.g., Deckop, 1988; Hirschey and Pappas, 1981; Jensen and Murphy, 1990). But, again, the re-

Shawn Berman

search findings on this front are hardly unequivocal, as others have found either that firm size is more important in determining compensation (e.g., Kostiuk, 1990) or that there is no relationship at all (Kerr and Bettis, 1987). The mixed results presented add to the supposition that the way in which compensation is computed can affect the findings (Gomez-Mejia, 1994). Gomez-Mejia (1994) further suggests that one reason for the weak cumulative results in the pay-performance literature is that managers are accountable to stakeholders other than shareholders. From this perspective the weak results presented in this study are somewhat disappointing, given the expanded the definition of performance employed here.

Finally, organizational size was the one variable to attain statistical significance in all three models. Unfortunately, interpreting this finding is hardly straightforward. First, given the methodology employed in this study, causality is not clear. Do firms that are most efficient at distributing resources to important stakeholders gain market share through cost leadership, or do large firms simply have more resources to ensure stakeholder satisfaction? It may also be that the variables used to compute the performance measure are biased, such that large firms will tend to have higher efficiency ratings in the DEA. Alternatively, stakeholders may be more willing to invest in long-term relationships with established firms, which leads to higher performance through gains associated with high levels of mutual trust. This relationship clearly warrants more study to determine if it is an empirical reality. If so, the factors underlying this finding also deserve further investigation.

The main lesson for practicing managers seems relatively simple. Firms that pay their CEOs in excess of industry norms may jeopardize important relationships with key stakeholders. As Donaldson and Preston (1995) explain in their treatment of instrumental stakeholder theory, managerial actions have consequences for specific stakeholder groups. Managers seeking to develop stakeholder relationships which lead to the long-run advantages of trust (e.g., lower contracting costs [Shapiro, Sheppard, and Cheraskin, 1992], and being perceived as a preferred trading partner [Barney and Hansen, 1994]), should avoid firms which devote an inappropriate share of resources to managerial compensation. Similarly, stakeholders that are locked into relationships with specific firms should consider all forms of managerial compensation as a sign of the firm's level of commitment in dealing fairly with all of its constituents.

Areas for Future Research and Conclusions
This research represents a tentative step toward adding empirical rigor to stakeholder theory, and expanding work linking pay and performance beyond the use of strictly financial measures. The findings presented here lend support to the ideas advanced within instrumental stakeholder theory. Organizations compensating managers well above the industry average per-

form less well. This work, therefore, not only buttresses the principles developed by stakeholder theorists, but relates to the work on trust between managers and stakeholders which suggests that self-serving actions by managers will erode the atmosphere of mutual respect necessary for above-average performance.

As is usual with such research, more questions are raised than answered. The causal nature of the relationship between compensation and performance should be explored. Do CEOs gradually entrench themselves, working to divert a greater share of firm resources to their own enrichment? Or, are poorly performing firms more susceptible to opportunistic managers? Also worthy of further study is the role of CEO characteristics in mediating and moderating this relationship. For example, Hill and Phan (1991) found tenure to be related to CEO compensation. It could be that long-term CEOs can insulate themselves from stakeholder attempts to rein-in self-serving managerial behavior. While some board characteristics were used in calculating the performance measure used in this study, further investigation of the board's role in approving seemingly unwarranted pay packages would yield additional insights into this phenomenon.

The link between firm size and performance also deserves further attention. This relationship may be due to a moderating factor, such as firm age. The wood products industry seems well suited for such a study because of the number of firms it contains, and the diversity in their ages. Again, the causal nature of this relationship should be investigated.

An obvious extension of this study would involve other industries. Additionally, surveys of stakeholder groups, so that stakeholder satisfaction could be included as an output variable in DEA calculations, would add to the face validity of the measure. Finally, case studies of both high- and low-performing firms would help answer many of the questions elaborated above. They could also serve to inform managers and organizational scholars of the traits of firms that both succeed and fail in distributing organizational resources to stakeholders in the most efficient manner.

This study undertook two major objectives: to use Data Envelopment Analysis (DEA) to construct a multidimensional measure of performance encompassing a variety of stakeholders, and to use this performance measure to assess the relationship between CEO compensation and firm performance. DEA holds much promise for scholars of social issues who are interested in exploring measures of performance that capture firm effects across a number of stakeholder groups. The results of regression analyses are broadly supportive of the propositions advanced by Jones (1995) in his development of instrumental stakeholder theory. The finding that excessive managerial compensation is negatively related to firm performance would seem to have far reaching implications for both managers and organizational scholars. This result should be subjected to further empirical investigation, but sug-

Shawn Berman

gests that managers must be mindful of the effects of short-term, self-interested behavior.

Shawn Berman (*shberman@bu.edu*) is Assistant Professor in Management Policy at the Boston University School of Management, 595 Commonwealth Avenue, Boston, MA 02215. This research report summarizes his doctoral dissertation research completed in 1998 at the University of Washington under the direction of Thomas M. Jones.

[1] The TLCS function in LIMDEP assumes that the coefficient vector is constant over time for all firms and controls for group-wise heteroskedasticity, cross-group correlation and within-group autocorrelation. Additionally, the model estimated here was a first-order autoregressive process (AR[1]) model.

References

Aoki, M. 1984. *The cooperative game theory of the firm*. Oxford: Clarendon Press.

Barney, J.B., and Hansen, M.H. 1994. Trustworthiness as a source of competitive advantage. *Strategic Management Journal*, 15 (Winter): 175-190.

Berle, A.A., and Means, G.C. 1932. *The modern corporation and private property*. New York: Macmillan.

Bendheim, C.L., Waddock, S.A., and Graves, S.B. 1998. Determining best practice in corporate-stakeholder relations using Data Envelopment Analysis: An industry-level study. *Business & Society*, 37 (3): 306-338.

Calton, J.M. 1996. Legitimizing stakeholder voice: The normative argument for institutionalizing moral discourse. In *Proceedings of the Seventh Annual Meeting of the International Association for Business and Society held in Santa Fe, NM, 21-24 March 1996*, ed. J.M. Logsdon and K. Rehbein: 555-560.

Calton, J.M., and Kurland, N.B. 1996. A theory of stakeholder enabling: Giving voice to the emerging praxis of organizational discourse. In *Postmodern management and organizational theory*, ed. D. Boje, R. Gephart, Jr., and T.J. Thatchenkery: 154-177. Thousand Oaks, CA: Sage Publications.

Calton, J.M., and Lad, L.J. 1995. Social contracting as a trust-building process of network governance. *Business Ethics Quarterly*, 5 (2): 271-296.

Charnes, A., Cooper, W.W., Lewin, A.Y., and Seiford, L.M. 1994. *Data Envelopment Analysis: Theory, methodology, and application*. Boston: Kluwer Academic.

Clarkson, M.B.E. 1995. A stakeholder framework for analyzing and evaluating corporate social performance. *Academy of Management Review*, 20 (1) (Jan.): 92-117.

Cyert, R.M., and March, J.G. 1963. *A behavioral theory of the firm*. Englewood Cliffs, NJ: Prentice-Hall.

Davis, G. 1991. Agents without principles? The spread of the poison pill throughout the corporate network. *Administrative Science Quarterly*, 36 (4) (Dec.): 583-613.

Deckop, J.R. 1988. Determinants of chief executive officer compensation. *Industrial and Labor Relations Review*, 41 (2) (Jan.): 215-226.

Donaldson, T., and Preston, L.E. 1995. The stakeholder theory of the corporation: Concepts, evidence, and implications. *Academy of Management Review*, 20 (1): 65-91.

Evan, W.M., and Freeman, R.E. 1993. A stakeholder theory of the modern corporation: Kantian capitalism. In *Ethical theory and business*, ed. T.L. Beauchamp and N.E. Bowie: 75-84. Englewood Cliffs, NJ: Prentice-Hall.

Frank, R. 1988. *Passions within reason: The strategic role of emotions*. New York: Norton.

Freeman, R.E. 1984. *Strategic management: A stakeholder approach*. Boston: Pitman.

Freeman, R.E. 1994. The politics of stakeholder theory: Some future directions. *Business Ethics Quarterly*, 4 (4): 409-421.

Gomez-Mejia, L.R. 1994. Executive compensation: A reassessment and a future research agenda. *Research in Personnel and Human Resources Management*, 12: 161-222.

Greene, B. 1992. *LIMDEP, version 6.0*. New York, NY: Econometric Studies Inc.

Griffin, J.J., and Mahon, J.F. 1997. The corporate social performance and corporate financial performance debate: Twenty-five years of incomparable research. *Business & Society*, 36 (1): 5-31.

Herman, E.S. 1981. *Corporate control, corporate power*. Cambridge, England: Cambridge University Press.

Hill, C.W.L. 1990. Cooperation, opportunism, and the invisible hand: Implications for transaction cost theory. *Academy of Management Review*, 15 (3): 500-513.

Hill, C.W.L. 1995. National institutional structures, transaction cost economizing and competitive advantage: The case of Japan. *Organizational Science*, 6 (1): 119-131.

Hill, C.W.L., and Phan, P. 1991. CEO tenure as a determinant of CEO pay. *Academy of Management Journal*, 34 (3): 712-717.

Hirschey, M., and Pappas, J.L. 1981. Regulatory and life cycle influences on managerial incentives. *Southern Economic Journal*, 48 (2): 327-334.

Howard, L., and Miller, J. 1993. Fair pay for fair play: Estimating pay equity in professional baseball with Data Envelopment Analysis. *Academy of Management Journal*, 36 (4): 882-894.

Jensen, M.C., and Meckling, W.H. 1976. Theory of the firm: Managerial behavior, agency costs, and ownership structure. *Journal of Financial Economics*, 3 (4): 305-360.

Jensen, M.C., and Murphy, K.J. 1990. Performance and top management incentives. *Journal of Political Economy*, 98 (2): 225-264.

Jones, T.M. 1995. Instrumental stakeholder theory: A synthesis of ethics and economics. *Academy of Management Review*, 20 (2): 404-437.

Kerr, J., and Bettis, R.A. 1987. Boards of directors, top management compensation, and shareholder returns. *Academy of Management Journal*, 30 (4): 745-764.

Kosnik, R.D. 1987. Greenmail: A study of board performance in corporate governance. *Administrative Science Quarterly*, 32 (2): 163-185.

Kostiuk, P.F. 1990. Firm size and executive compensation. *Journal of Human Relations*, 25 (1): 90-105.

Lewicki, R.J., and Bunker, B.B. 1996. Developing and maintaining trust in work relationships. In *Trust in organizations: Frontiers of theory and research*, ed. R.M. Kramer and T.R. Tyler: 114-139. Thousand Oaks, CA: Sage.

Marris, R. 1964. *The economic theory of managerial capitalism*. New York: Macmillan.

Meyer, J.W., and Rowan, B. 1977. Institutionalized organizations: Formal structures as myth and ceremony. *American Journal of Sociology*, 83 (2): 340-363.

Neter, J., Wasserman,W. and Kutner, M.H. 1989. *Applied regression models.* Homewood, IL: Irwin.

Ring, P.S., and Van de Ven, A.H. 1992. Structuring cooperative relationships between organizations. *Strategic Management Journal*, 13 (7): 483-498.

Shapiro, D.L., Sheppard, B.H., and Cheraskin, L. 1992. Business on a handshake. *Negotiation Journal*, 8 (4): 365-377.

Sloan, A. 1996. The hit men. *Newsweek*, Feb. 26: 44-48.

Solomon, R.C. 1992. *Ethics and excellence: Cooperation and integration in business.* New York: Oxford University Press.

Steers, R.M., and Ungson, G.R. 1987. Strategic issues in executive compensation decisions. In *New perspectives on compensation*, ed. D.B. Balkin and L.R. Gomez-Mejia: 315-327. Englewood Cliffs, NJ: Prentice-Hall.

Tukey, J.W. 1977. *Exploratory data analysis.* Reading, MA: Addison-Wesley.

Ungson, G.R., and Steers, R.M. 1984. Motivation and politics in executive compensation. *Academy of Management Review*, 9 (2): 313-323.

Weick, K. 1979. Cognitive processes in organizations. *Research in Organizational Behavior*, 1: 41-74.

An Independent Social Audit/External Assessment of Levi Strauss

Kim Davenport, Fielding Institute

Introduction

Social auditing has historically been undertaken from one of two perspectives: from the inside, assessing a company's performance against its stated objectives, or from the outside, evaluating its performance in relation to other organizations' behavior and social norms. This paper summarizes a social audit performed using content analysis of information in the public domain. An assessment is provided of Levi Strauss's social performance compared to twenty Principles of Corporate Citizenship (Davenport, 1998). The assessment covers three broad categories of principles. These principles emanated from research (Davenport, 1998) that explored how stakeholders define corporate citizenship and how social auditing can be used as a tool for assessing it.

The 1998 study used Delphi methodology to arrive at consensus statements among stakeholder experts. The Delphi method allows input from a diverse set of participants about expectations of corporate behavior. The three categories of principles, along with their operational principles, are shown in Figure 1.

Social Audit of Levi Strauss

I. Ethical Business Behavior

According to Robert Haas (Haas, 1997: 17), CEO of Levi Strauss, companies traditionally approach ethics in one of three ways; that is, with:

1. Neglect or the absence of any formal ethical programs.
2. Compliance-based programs.
3. Values-oriented programs.

Haas adds that Levi Strauss takes the third approach by combining company/functional values with individual responsibility and accountability. Specifically, the company is guided by a commitment to considering the impacts of its decisions on stakeholders using six ethical principles:

honesty, promise-keeping, fairness, respect for others, compassion, and integrity. Haas, the great-great-grandnephew of founder Levi Strauss, explains:

> We address ethical issues by first identifying which of these principles applies to the particular business decision. Then, we determine which internal and external stakeholders' ethical concerns should influence our business decisions. We are integrating ethics with our other corporate values, including diversity, open communications, empowerment recognition, teamwork and honesty, into every aspect of our business (Haas, 1997: 18).

Levi's Aspirations statement is at the core of its Ethical Principles. Created in 1987, it explains the type of company both management and employees are trying to create (Levi Strauss, 1997a): a company that people are proud of and committed to, one where all employees have an opportunity to contribute, learn, grow and advance based on merit, not policies or background, and with an environment where people feel respected, are treated fairly, are listened to and involved. The statement says, "Above all, we want satisfaction from accomplishments and friendships, balanced personal and professional lives, and to have fun in our endeavors" (Levi Strauss, 1997a).

Also included in the Aspirations statement is an acknowledgment of a desire to build on the company's past. An excerpt from the statement illuminates this point: today's employees hope to "[affirm] the best of [the] Company's traditions, [close] gaps that may exist between principles and practices, and [update] values to reflect contemporary circumstances"(Levi Strauss, 1997a).

Six leadership characteristics are described as being necessary to make the Aspirations a reality (Levi Strauss, 1997a):

1. Teamwork and Trust
2. Diversity
3. Recognition
4. Ethical Management Practices
5. Communications
6. Empowerment

The company also has a Code of Ethics and sometimes publishes specific guidelines, policies and procedures to guide ethical behavior. It also relies on its Principled Reasoning Approach, which is a rational process to determine the ethical impacts of behavior on key groups of constituents. An example of how Levi employees used the Principled Reasoning Approach was in the creation of two global ethics policies (Solomon, 1996: 73). The "Terms of Engagement" policy provides operating guidelines to address workplace issues with its business partners throughout the world. As described by Solomon (1996: 74), the Terms of Engagement were created in 1992, and address health and safety issues, wages, discrimination, child labor,

Figure 1:   Corporate Citizenship Principles

I.	*Ethical business behavior is exemplified by a company that:*	
	P1.	Engages in fair and honest business practices in its relationships with stake-holders.
	P2.	Sets high standards of behavior for all employees.
	P3.	Exercises ethical oversight at the executive and board levels.
II.	*Stakeholder commitment is demonstrated when the company:*	
	P4.	Is "well-managed" for all stakeholders.
	P5.	Initiates and engages in genuine dialogue with stakeholders.
	P6.	Values and implements disclosure.
II.A.	*Stakeholder commitment to Communities (global & local) is demonstrated when the company:*	
	P7.	Fosters a reciprocal relationship between the corporation and community.
	P8.	Invests in the communities in which it operates.
II.B.	*Stakeholder commitment to Consumers is demonstrated when the company:*	
	P9.	Respects the rights of consumers.
	P10.	Offers quality products and services.
	P11.	Provides information that is truthful and useful.
II.C.	*Stakeholder commitment to Employees is demonstrated when the company:*	
	P12.	Provides a family-friendly work environment.
	P13.	Engages in responsible human resource management.
	P14.	Provides an equitable reward and wage system for employees.
	P15.	Engages in open and flexible communications with employees.
	P16.	Invests in employee development.
II.D.	*Stakeholder commitment to Investors is demonstrated when the company:*	
	P17.	Strives for a competitive return on investment.
II.E.	*Stakeholder commitment to Suppliers is demonstrated when the company:*	
	P18.	Engages in fair trading practices with suppliers.
III.	*Environmental commitment is demonstrated when the company:*	
	P19.	Demonstrates a commitment to the environment.
	P20.	Demonstrates a commitment to sustainable development.

conditions of suppliers facilities and environmental protection. The second policy, "Country Assessment Guidelines," deals with human rights issues, political stability, safety for company employees, and legal protection of trademarks and commercial interests (Levi Strauss, 1998).

Ethical behavior is also encouraged through the employee evaluation and reward system. Employees are evaluated by their supervisors and their peers to determine how well they perform on ethical issues and other business goals (Solomon, 1996: 73).

Levi's April 1996, $4.3 billion buy-back of nearly one-third of the company's publicly held stock is yet another demonstration of its commitment to ethical behavior. The leveraged buy-out transferred control over the company's governance to a four-person voting trust: Haas; his uncle Peter Haas, Sr.; cousin Peter Haas, Jr.; and Warren Hellmann, a distant relation who is a partner in Hellmann and Friedman, a San Francisco investment banking firm (Sherman, 1997: 106).

To ensure that family stewards could run the company as they saw fit, Sherman (1997: 106), notes that "the SEC [Securities and Exchange Commission] document describing the transaction states that those who choose to remain shareholders must 'make an explicit commitment to the values currently articulated and practiced by the company.'" In addition, the SEC document specifies that "the voting trust 'will permit management to run the company in a manner consistent with the company's Mission and Aspirations Statement and Business Vision.'"

Assessment of Ethical Business Behavior
Three principles *(P1, P2, P3)* define ethical business behavior.

Levi Strauss clearly adheres to the first two ethical principles. It *engages in fair and honest business practices in its relationships with stakeholders (P1),* and *sets high standards of behavior for all employees (P2)*. The company's use of the Principled Reasoning Approach to decision-making demonstrates its integration of ethics into day-to-day work, especially in considering the impact of decisions on stakeholders. The Terms of Engagement support Levi's ethical values, while being fair and honest with its business partners. Employees are given extensive training to ensure they understand how ethics apply to their work environment, and they are also evaluated and compensated according to their adherence to the company's ethical values.

Because the company is now privately controlled, the literal interpretation of *P3*, that the company *exercises ethical oversight at the executive and board levels*, is not so clear-cut. However, the spirit of the principle, i.e., ethical governance practices, is certainly exhibited by the decision to buy-back public stock at a premium price so that the family could govern the company more consistently with its values rather than catering to the whims of Wall Street.

Based on the literature reviewed for this study, Levi Strauss appears to be exemplary, striving to adhere to ethical principles it has established for itself and that are consistent with the principles identified in this research.

II. Stakeholder Commitment
Levi's efforts to manage the company for the benefit of all stakeholders is best demonstrated by the Principled Reasoning Approach to decision-making. At its core, Principled Reasoning calls for thinking through the impacts decisions have on stakeholders. In this process, information on stakeholder issues is compiled. Possible recommendations are then discussed directly with the "high influence" stakeholder groups, thus fostering genuine dialogue with stakeholders (Haas, 1997: 18).

Levi's Global Sourcing Guidelines, described by Levi's CEO, serve as an example:

To develop the guidelines, we formed a working group made up of

Kim Davenport

fifteen employees from a broad cross-section of the company. The working group spent nine months at the task, during which time its members researched views of key stakeholder groups–sewing-machine operators, vendors, contractors, plant managers, merchandisers, contract productions staff, shareholders and others. The working group then used an ethical decision-making model to guide its deliberations. The model is a process for making decisions by taking into consideration all stakeholders' issues (Haas, 1994: 13).

In addition to annually producing documents like the Levi Strauss Foundation Report (e.g., Levi Strauss, 1992 and 1996), describing Levi's community involvement and its philanthropic donations, the company also provides information regarding its environmental performance and conducts audits of its suppliers to ensure conformance to labor policies. Since implementing the policies in 1992, audit teams have visited suppliers on an annual basis to determine whether their facilities and working conditions adhere to the company's policies. The first audits indicated that "70 percent of the contractors were in compliance, 25 percent needed improvements, and 5 percent chose to no longer supply the company" (Baron, 1995: 80).

Assessment of Commitment to Stakeholders
Levi Strauss meets all three criteria of good corporate citizenship in the Commitment to Stakeholders category, *P4*, *P5*, and *P6*. The extent to which Levi Strauss utilizes the Principled Reasoning Approach to incorporate the views and assess the ethical concerns of suppliers, stockholders, employees and other stakeholders, points to its efforts at *managing the company for the benefit of all stakeholders (P4)*. Levi has also consistently demonstrated its willingness to *initiate and engage in genuine dialogue with stakeholders (P5)* through the processes it uses to develop policies (and through the policies themselves). Finally, the company demonstrates that it *values and implements disclosure (P6)* by the information it releases and the audits it willingly and voluntarily undertakes.

Skeptics have questioned whether Levi's success is really due to the company's ethical foundation and its inclusion of stakeholders viewpoints, or if its "great wealth, derived from the happy accident of owning a mythic brand, permits the luxury of genteel behavior" (Sherman, 1997: 108). Whatever the source of its behavior, Levi's performance speaks to its commitment to its stakeholders.

II. A. Community Commitment
Consistent with *P7, fostering a reciprocal relationship between the corporation and community*, Levi has a Community Involvement Team program. The program recognizes employee volunteerism, and awards grants to community projects identified and actively supported by Levi Strauss employees and

retiree teams (Willis, 1986: 51). According to the Levi Strauss Foundation Report (1992: 4), Levi also has Employee Giving Programs for organizations such as the United Way. This report describes other workplace contribution programs, gift-matching programs, and community service programs that are also available to employees. In addition, employees are given the opportunity to play a significant role in the design and implementation of Levi Strauss Foundation programs.

P8, the company *invests in the communities in which it operates,* is addressed in a variety of ways. First, the Levi Strauss Foundation has an annual giving goal of 2.5 percent of pre-tax profits. The Foundation's Community Partnership Programs (Levi Strauss, 1996: 3) have goals of working with poor and under-served people; taking the lead in addressing difficult social issues; and supporting non-profit organizations that contribute important ideas and technical expertise to Levi's grant-making areas of interest. Addressing the needs of disadvantaged and under-served people is done through work in community-based economic development, AIDS prevention and care, and social justice.

Levi's most recent accolade for community involvement, in January 1998, came from the White House in the form of the Ron Brown Award for Corporate Leadership. A newswire story reported that Levi Strauss was recognized for its "Project Change" initiative, a broad-based program that addresses racial prejudice and institutional racism in communities where the company operates. The program is aimed at dismantling institutional policies and practices that promote discrimination, easing tensions between majority and minority groups and promoting diversity in community organizations. "Project Change" was specifically cited for effectively linking a diverse coalition of community organizations to improve race relations in those communities (Anonymous, 1998).

In 1998, Levi had an opportunity to demonstrate its community commitment. Eleven factory closures in four states and Canada involved the lay off of 6,395 employees (34 percent of its manufacturing workforce in the United States and Canada). In an unprecedented move, described by journalist Michael Verespej (1998: 24), "[Levi] . . . unveiled an unheard-of $200 million employee benefits plan to help ease laid-off workers through the transition." In addition, the communities affected by the plant closures were granted $8 million over three years to ease the social and economic impact of the closures. Because the company was concerned about its impact on the local communities, it remained active after the plant closures and sought ways to strengthen the local economic and industrial base (Verespej, 1998).

Assessment of Commitment to Community
By the standards established in this research study, Levi would be considered a good corporate citizen in the area of community commitment. The

company *fosters a reciprocal relationship between the company and community (P7)* by encouraging employee volunteerism and input regarding the programs its Foundation supports. The company *invests in communities where it operates (P8)* by encouraging community-based economic development, and gets involved in difficult social issues ranging from AIDS prevention to racial discrimination. If business reasons mandate plant closures, the communities impacted are provided financial support to aid their recoveries.

II. B. Consumer Commitment

Levi's historic financial success and its recent economic downturns have been attributed to consumer-related issues, i.e., good products, good marketing and good distribution, or the lack thereof. Since 1984, when Haas took over, the company has become consumer-driven, shifting its emphasis from manufacturing to marketing. The shift has proven to be a winner. During the first decade of Robert Haas's tenure, Levi's revenue tripled and net income multiplied eighteen times–to $735 million at the end of 1995 (Sherman, 1997: 112).

Levi's brand marketing has been "first-rate." Though the company sells pants of various styles to consumers of all ages, Levi targets its advertising at youngsters aged fifteen to nineteen, and nearly always promotes its "501" jeans. Until 1984, Levi brands were mostly sold to customers in the western American states, but 501s now account for approximately 33 percent of Levi's domestic jeans sales (Sherman, 1997: 114).

Levi pioneered mass retail customization with its Personal Pair jeans program. In an effort to be more customer focused, Levi is now tailoring its products to individual specification. "Mass-customized products are assembled-to-order from available components on highly agile production lines" (Reda, 1996: 37). Obviously, innovation and marketing go "hand-in-hand" at Levi's.

Despite its many successes, Levi does have an "Achilles heel": its relationship with distributors. Not long ago, the company took as long as sixty days to ship orders, missing untold sales opportunities and no doubt frustrating distributors (Sherman, 1997: 116). Realizing its manufacturing and distribution were weak areas, Levi undertook an ambitious and costly reengineering effort. It has taken six years and $850 million to restructure its relationships with distributors and suppliers. But in February 1997, its pilot program with the May Company was said to be paying off with more accurate forecasts and improvements in supply lines (Abend, 1997: 20).

The turnaround may be too late. The company's exorbitant restructuring investment, intense competition from designer jeans markets, and lost market share to lower-priced private-label and mass marketed brands are thought to have caused Levi's massive employment cutbacks and plant closures. Simply put, the company may have been slow to react. It took too long to tighten its belt and shrink its United States-based manufacturing to reflect its efficiency gains and decreased market share. Critics argue (Mariotti, 1998: 82) that "Levi fell asleep at the wheel" in both the consumer and customer front, and its employees and communities have suffered most as a result of this mismanagement.

Assessment of Commitment to Consumers
No issues related to consumer rights were uncovered is this assessment. Given the company's ethical commitment and codes of conduct, privacy issues and solicitation problems seem unlikely. It can safely be assumed that Levi *respects the rights of its consumers (P9)*.

Levi certainly *offers quality products and services (P10)*. The product is famous for its durability. Levi's advertising has been exemplary, easily meeting the criteria of *P11*, which requires the company to *provide information that is truthful and useful*.

Taking a literal interpretation of the principles, Levi gets a "good corporate citizenship" rating in this area. However, the principles don't directly address basic good management–which could be called the spirit of consumer commitment. And that is where Levi has fallen short. Poor distribution and miscalculation of consumer taste caused the company to lose sales and market share. In the spirit of consumer commitment, Levi has at least temporarily "stubbed its toe."

II. C. Employee Commitment
Levi's commitment to employees in good and bad times dates back to the Depression. Rather than laying off Levi workers, Walter Haas Sr., CEO at the time, put employees on short work weeks, and paid them to lay new floors at the Valencia Street plant in San Francisco until demand for products recovered (Levi Strauss, 1997b). Years later, in the 1980s, when market declines in the United States forced the company to close plants and lay off more than a third of its work force, policies were developed to "help former employees make the transition to new jobs and to cushion the adverse impact of plant closures on communities" (Levi Strauss, 1997b).

In June of 1996, times were good for Levi Strauss. The company announced plans to reward its 37,500 employees worldwide with a one-time bonus equal to about a year's pay if Levi met its performance goals by the year 2001 (Goff, 1997: 34). The offering was valued at $750 million. The plan was by far the largest incentive the company had ever offered, and certainly stood high above any of its peers. Then Labor Secretary, Robert Reich, lauded the bonus package for sharing gains with those in the boardroom and on the factory floor (Groves, 1996: 1A).

But job security proved to be elusive even for an icon like Levi Strauss. The antithesis of the millennium bonus plan occurred in the fall of 1997 when Levi announced that eleven plants would close and approximately 6,400 American employees would be laid off (Verespej, 1998: 24).

In spite of making the tough downsizing decision, the company's compassion and generosity remained steadfast, with a $200 million severance package. Michael Verespej, senior editor for *Industry Week* (1998: 24) describes the package:

> Each laid-off employee received up to three weeks' severance pay for each year of service, eight months' pay from the date of the announcement, outplacement and career-counseling services. What's more, workers were given the entire severance package even if they immediately found new jobs. Levi Strauss also provided company-paid health-care benefits for up to 18 months and up to $6,000 per worker for education, job training, and/or moving expenses (Verespej, 1998: 24).

True to its stakeholder commitment, Levi worked closely with its unions to develop the severance package for all affected workers. Union officials described it as the richest severance package ever offered in the apparel industry. Executive Vice President, Bruce Raynor, of the Union of Needletrades, Industrial and Textile Employees (UNITE), commented: "The bottom line is that workers still lose their jobs and we regret that, but I think the company really stepped up here and did everything [it] could, within reason, to soften the blow" (Hill, 1998: 34).

Although the union encouraged Levi to cut back its off-shore sourcing, union leaders acknowledged that they were pleased (given the impact of the North American Free Trade Agreement (NAFTA) and competitors like Tommy Hilfiger) that Levi made a commitment to retain 55 percent of its production in the United States and Canada (Hill, 1998: 33).

In a November 1997 speech at the Business for Social Responsibility (BSR) annual conference, Haas described the difficult decision to close factories. He explained that, from a strictly financial perspective, the plants should have been closed several years ago. But because the company was privately controlled and strongly believed the values stated in its Aspirations statement and Ethical Principles, the decision was delayed in hopes of an economic turnaround. When that turnaround failed to materialize, the inevitable occurred.

One area that is consistently above average is the Levi employee benefits package. Employees have access to services that few companies come close to matching. Two years in a row, *Money* magazine named Levi the company with the best employee benefits in the United States. In 1995, Levi became the first Fortune 500 company to offer full medical benefits to all unmarried partners of its employees (Groves, 1996: 1A). Paid vacations are especially generous: three weeks for new employees, and seven weeks after twenty years' service. As described by *Los Angeles Times* journalist, Martha Groves (1996: 1A), Levi also has "flexible time-off policies (including Friday afternoons off during summer months), to help employees balance their work and personal lives." Other examples of company benefits include a Prenatal Program, an Employee Assistance Program (EAP), and a childcare voucher system.

Levi's employee programs are not without controversy, according to journalist, Jennifer Laabs. Laabs reports (1997: 17) that in 1997, the company lost a $10.6 million lawsuit over a contested return-to-work program. Five plaintiffs maintained that rather than facilitating their return to work, the program actually intimidated them so they'd quit. An eleven-member El Paso County (Texas) jury found Levi Strauss guilty and ordered the company to pay the plaintiffs over $600,000 in compensatory damages. It also awarded them $10 million in punitive damages. The company is appealing the decision.

Levi, in its defense, described its program as an attempt to re-integrate employees into the workforce after extended periods of absence, and assured jurors that employees were not asked to join the program until their doctor gave them a clean bill of health. The company is appealing the judgment (Laabs, 1997:17-18).

Assessment of Commitment to Employees

Five principles, *P12* to *P16*, determine a firm's commitment to employees. In spite of the back-to-work lawsuit, Levi Strauss appears to warrant an "A" when it comes employee relations. The company *provides a family-friendly work environment (P12)* by offering daycare, eldercare, prenatal and lactational programs to help employees balance their work and personal lives. It demonstrated *responsible human resource management (P13)* with the severance and retraining packages associated with its plant closures. The millennium bonus package set a new standard for *providing an equitable reward and wage system for employees (P14)*. Employee involvement in decision-making about the company's philanthropy and community involvement, as well as re-engineering efforts to streamline the company's operations, are examples of *engaging employees in open and flexible communications (P15)*. Levi demonstrates its willingness to *invest in employee development (P16)* by offering programs such as ethics training, leadership development, and retraining.

II. D. Investor Commitment

An article in *Fortune* magazine (Sherman, 1997: 104) describes Levi Strauss as "a champion wealth creator." The article cites Levi as the global leader in branded apparel, ranking fifteenth among *Fortune*'s most admired corporations. Under CEO Robert Haas, it points out, Levi's shares rose from $2.53, adjusted for stock splits, to $265 (the value reported to the SEC as part of a

1996 recapitalization).

Journalist Andrée Conrad (1997: 20) reported that Levi Strauss produced sales of $7.1 billion in 1996, up 6 percent from 1995: $4.3 billion in the United States and $2.8 billion offshore. Struggling to get its costs in line, Levi announced in early 1997 that it would shave $80 million from its annual operating costs by eliminating 1,000 salaried American jobs. Upon closer evaluation, the impacts of the cuts were softened, since early retirement eliminated roughly 250 of the 1,000 positions. It wasn't until late in 1997 that Levi cut to the bone when it decided to close the eleven American factories and eliminate 6,000 positions.

This decision was not a "knee-jerk" reaction, but one that, from a financial perspective, was long overdue. CEO Haas explained the delay:

> Everyone looks at the wrong end of the telescope, as if profits drive the business. . . . Financial reporting doesn't get to the real stuff-employee morale, turnover, consumer satisfaction, on-time delivery, consumer attitudes, perceptions of the brand, purchase intentions-that drives financial results. I believe that if you create an environment that your people identify with, that is responsive to their sense of values, justice, fairness, ethics, compassion, and appreciation, they will help you be successful (Sherman, 1997: 106).

It would be hard for investors to dispute that view. Since 1984 when Haas became CEO, Levi's financial performance has been an investor's dream. Sherman explains:

> By April [of 1996], the company had increased its total market value roughly 14-fold. . . . The retirement of millions of shares of stock-some 30 percent of the total outstanding . . . dramatically boost[ed] per share returns. At the same time, the deal reduced the total value of Levi Strauss by the $4 billion that was paid out in cash to shareholders. But plain, old-fashioned net income . . . multiplied by a very handsome 18 times during Haas' tenure. (Sherman, 1997: 112).

Haas attributes much of the company's sustained growth to its freedom from Wall Street's demands for short-term results. Haas (Conrad, 1997: 20) explains: "Private ownership . . . has given [Levi Strauss] more freedom to focus on long-term brand building, corporate social responsibility and community involvement. . . . It's given us the continuing ability to follow a path that will have its ups and downs-but our success will be measured in decades, not quarterly snapshots."

Investors' long-term earning potential has certainly been affected by two areas: the massive re-engineering effort, costing $850 million and taking six years to implement (Abend, 1997: 20), and the fact that the company has lost market share because it lost sight of consumer taste. Regarding the first, after much disruption and stress, the pilot program has just begun to show improvements in the company distribution and forecasting efforts. More complex is the issue of consumer taste. Both of these management issues have been legitimate reasons for investors to "raise eyebrows."

Assessment of Commitment to Investors
One principle, *P17*, demonstrates commitment to investors. Over the last decade, Levi Strauss has consistently provided a *competitive return on investment (P17)* while trying to balance the needs of all of its key stakeholders. Nonetheless, its financial performance has recently hit upon "rocky times," with high cost structures and loss of market share. At the time of this audit, Levi's financial performance looks "bearish."

II. E. Supplier Commitment
Levi's relationship with suppliers is navigated by its Global Sourcing and Operating Guidelines. This comprehensive guide is comprised of two policies (Levi Strauss, 1998):

1. The Business Partner Terms of Engagement deal with issues that are substantially controllable by Levi Strauss's individual business partners.
2. The Country Assessment Guidelines address larger, external issues that help the company assess the risk of doing business in a particular country.

Described on the Levi Strauss website (Levi Strauss, 1998), the policies were created to help the company select business partners who follow workplace standards and business practices consistent with Levi policies. They apply to every contractor that manufactures or finishes products for Levi Strauss. Trained auditors monitor compliance among nearly 500 cutting, sewing, and finishing contractors in over fifty countries. The goal of the resource-intensive effort is to achieve positive results and effect change, not to punish transgressing contractors. Through its guidelines, the company hopes to find long-term solutions that benefit the individuals who make its products and to enhance the quality of life in their communities.

Assessment of Commitment to Suppliers
One principle, *P18*, summarizes a company's commitment to suppliers. The policies that guide Levi's relationship with suppliers seek to ensure that the company *engages in fair trading practices (P18)*. Levi's relationship with its suppliers is consistent with the principles established by stakeholders and used in this study.

III. Environmental Commitment

In spite of overall progress in the industry to reuse, recycle, and reduce waste, 68 percent of the respondents to a survey of American Apparel Manufacturing Association members reported that "landfills [are their] primary method of disposal for a staggering amount of waste" (Bonner, 1997: 60). Like its colleagues in the apparel industry, Levi faces several environmental challenges. First is how to reduce the millions of pounds of scrap the company produces each year. To decrease its dependence on landfills (which have extensive environmental and financial costs), Levi employs three familiar strategies: reduce, reuse and recycle (Bonner, 1997: 52). Bonner describes two of Levi's initiatives:

> In 1994, Levi Strauss implemented its Global Environmental Council, which includes representatives from every area of the company. Their efforts resulted in the firm's recycling 85% of its 14,000 tons of scrap produced annually.... [C]reative alternatives to the landfill [include using] denim scraps ... in construction materials, roofing tile, engine gaskets, insulation, car seats and doll stuffing. (Bonner, 1997: 58-59).

Also in 1994, Levi launched a partnership with paper manufacturer Crane & Co. to "[recycle] its denim scraps into 100% cotton paper for internal use as company letterhead, envelopes and corporate checks" (Anonymous, 1994). According to the latest reported results, 400,000 pounds of waste was recycled and the company had reduced paper costs by 12 percent (Anonymous, 1994).

The Global Sourcing Guidelines also provide environmental guidance for contractors and suppliers. To do business with Levi Strauss, suppliers must meet the environmental standards that the company has established. For example, one of Levi's Mexican contractors "now recycles 36% of the water used in its laundry and textiles facilities and an Italian finishing center recycles 60% of its water" (Bonner, 1997: 68).

However, challenges for the industry and Levi Strauss remain. There are no easy answers about how far Levi's environmental policies should extend into its supply chain. As an example, an unsolved issue is that Levi's subcontractors may do business with small laundries that don't have the technological capability to remove effluents (Baron, 1995: 80).

Assessment of Commitment to the Environment

Two principles, *P19* and *P20*, define environmental commitment. Levi has demonstrated its *commitment to the environment (P19)* through internal and contractor policies and by results–recycling 85 percent of its 14,000 tons of scrap and partnering with Crane to use scrap denim to make the firm's business cards and stationery. As significant an impact as Levi and the industry have had on the environment, I was surprised to find little written on the topic. Thus, it is not clear to me what effort Levi is making toward *sustainable development (P20)*.

Summary

Upon conclusion of this independent external social audit of Levi Strauss, it can safely be said that Levi Strauss meets, and often sets, a best-practice standard for good corporate citizenship. The benefit of this type of assessment is the establishment of criteria that allow inter-company comparisons of social performance. The information is also useful for individuals and organizations concerned about corporate social responsibility (e.g., social responsible investors and consumers).

Kim Davenport (*KimDavenp@aol.com*) (1421 Peachtree St., Atlanta, GA 30309) earned her Ph.D. at the Fielding Institute, Santa Barbara, CA, with an advisory committee chaired by Barbara Mink. This paper is based on her dissertation (Davenport, 1998).

References

Abend, J. 1997. Levi's, Claiborne, Kmart: Getting refocused. *Bobbin*, 38 (6) (Feb.): 20-23.

Anonymous. 1994. L.S. & Co. turns scrap denim into paper. *Apparel Industry Magazine*, 55 (3) (Mar.): 13.

Anonymous. 1998. IBM Corporation and Levi Strauss & Co. named winners of Ron Brown Award for Corporate Leadership. *PR Newswire*, Feb. 11.

Baron, D.P. 1995. The nonmarket strategy system. *Sloan Management Review*, 37 (1) (Fall): 73-85.

Bonner, S. 1997. It's not easy being green: Strategies and challenges. *Apparel Industry Magazine*, 58 (2) (Feb.): 52-62.

Conrad, A. 1997. The year profit became fashionable. *Apparel Industry Magazine*, 58 (6) (June): 20-38.

Davenport, K.S. 1998. *Corporate citizenship: A stakeholder approach for defining corporate social performance and identifying measures for assessing it*. Doctoral dissertation, The Fielding Institute, Santa Barbara, CA. Proquest, UMI, AAT 9839178.

Goff, J. 1997. An eye on the millennium. *CFO Magazine*, 13 (8) (Aug.): 34-41.

Groves, M. 1996. Levi Strauss offers year's pay as incentive bonus. *Los Angeles Times* [Home Edition], June 13: 1A.

Haas, R.D. 1994. Ethics in the trenches. *Across the Board*, 31 (5) (May): 12-13.

Haas, R.D. 1997. Business ethics. *Executive Excellence*, 14 (6) (June): 17-18.

Hill, S. 1998. Levi Strauss shrinks to fit U.S. market. *Apparel Industry Magazine*, 59 (1) (Jan.): 32-43.

Laabs, J.J. 1997. Levi Strauss loses $10.6 million lawsuit over contested return-to-work program. *Workforce*, 76 (11) (Nov.): 17-18.

Levi Strauss. [1992.] *Levi Strauss Foundation Report [for 1992].* [San Francisco: The Company.]

Levi Strauss. [1996.] *Levi Strauss Foundation Report [for 1996].* [San Francisco: The Company.]

Levi Strauss. 1997a. *Mission statement, aspirations statement, business vision, code of ethics and ethical principles.* [San Francisco: The Company.] [Internal company document, dated 7/11/97. Published on website, *All About Levi Strauss & Co.*, http://www.levistrauss.com, prior to Sept. 1999.]

Levi Strauss. 1997b. *Milestones: Levi Strauss & Co. history.* [San Francisco: The Company.] [Internal company document, dated 7/11/97. Published on website, *All About Levi Strauss & Co.*, http://www.levistrauss.com, prior to Sept. 1999.]

Levi Strauss. [c.1998.] Global sourcing & operating guidelines. *All About Levi Strauss & Co.. General Information: Code of Conduct.* http://www.levistrauss.com (c. May).

Mariotti, J. 1998. Icons at the brink. *Industry Week,* 247 (3) (Feb. 2): 82.

Reda, S. 1996. Mass customization retailing: Giving customers exactly what they want. *Stores,* 78 (6) (June): 37-39.

Sherman, S. 1997. Levi's: As ye sew, so shall ye reap. *Fortune,* 135 (9) (May 12): 104ff.

Solomon, C.M. 1996. Put your ethics to a global test. *Personnel Journal,* 75 (1) (Jan.): 66-74.

Verespej, M. 1998. How to manage adversity. *Industry Week,* 247 (2) (Jan. 19): 24.

Willis, R. 1986. The Levi Strauss credo: Fashion and philanthropy. *Management Review,* 75 (7) (July): 51-54.

Stakeholders and Corporate Performance Measures: An Impact Assessment

Jeanne M. Logsdon, University of New Mexico
Patsy Granger Lewellyn, University of South Carolina at Aiken

Introduction

Stakeholder theory has had major impacts in the field of business and society over the years since the publication of Freeman's seminal book in 1984 (Näsi, 1995; Clarkson, 1998). Increasingly, the language of stakeholders is used in corporate mission statements, executive communications, and public relations statements. Over the same period, another significant trend influencing business practice has been increasing competitive pressure to improve quality and increase efficiency. Corporate responses to this pressure include Total Quality Management (TQM) and re-engineering studies of factors affecting future revenues and profits. In addition, the scope of managerial information systems is expanding to include non-financial performance data, on topics such as customer satisfaction (Lynch and Cross, 1991; Kaplan and Norton, 1992). These data, not traditionally included in internal accounting systems, are labeled "new performance measures" in the accounting and strategy literatures.

The term, "stakeholder," has recently appeared in conjunction with recommendations for developing new performance measures for better strategic planning (Atkinson, Waterhouse, and Wells, 1997) and is used in advertising by at least one management consulting firm (Arthur Andersen, 1997: S5). To date, however, the actual impacts of stakeholder theory on performance measurement and corporate reporting have not been studied. But, the increasing use of stakeholder language is merely rhetoric unless and until companies institutionalize stakeholder interests into routine decision-making and reporting.

This research project examines the ways firms design non-financial performance measures, and, in particular, ways that incorporate the "stakeholder" concept. The project includes qualitative and quantitative components. Stages of the research described in this paper include a pilot survey of corporations and their performance measurement practices, and case studies of a small sample of companies demonstrating commitment to new corporate performance measurement.

Background

Growing Popularity of the "Stakeholder" Term

Freeman (1984) introduced modern stakeholder theory to the business and society field, and explicitly linked stakeholder interests to corporate strategy. Freeman's broad definition of a stakeholder as "any group or individual who can affect or is affected by the achievement of the organization's objectives" (1984: 46) is still widely used. By the end of the 1980s, the stakeholder concept was firmly embedded in the field, although the relationships between stakeholder theory and other fundamental concepts had not been fully worked out. The series of conferences on stakeholder theory, convened by Clarkson at the University of Toronto, spurred a number of conceptual developments that further strengthened the understanding and usefulness of the stakeholder concept (Clarkson, 1998; Jones, 1994). Today it is a core concept that permeates both research and teaching in the field. Other business disciplines have also discovered the "stakeholder" term and have begun to incorporate it in their research (e.g., Kotter and Heskett, 1992; Harrison and St. John, 1996).

While executives continue to be trained in the zero-sum trade-off language of economics and finance, they also recognize the interdependency of shareholder, customer, employee, and supplier interests. This view is consistent with the managerial view of the firm that addresses a narrow set of economically based stakeholders (Windsor, 1992; Carroll, 1996; Mitchell, Agle, and Wood, 1997).

An expanded view of stakeholders, advocated in the business and society literature, looks beyond the traditional market-based set of stakeholders recognized in the managerial view of the firm (i.e., owners, customers, employees, and suppliers). It includes all groups with salient claims on the firm, based upon the criteria of legitimacy, power, and/or urgency (Mitchell, Agle, and Wood, 1997). Normative, instrumental, and descriptive dimensions of stakeholder analysis can be included in this expanded perspective (Donaldson and Preston, 1995; Jones, 1995). Thus, the expanded stakeholder set could include local communities, special interest groups, units of government at various levels, the media, the general public, competitors, and others (Freeman, 1984; Carroll, 1996).

This broader stakeholder definition is more likely to be accepted by the business community if business and society scholars understand new performance measures. We will then be able to initiate discussion with scholars in other disciplines, and executives in the strategy and accounting areas, about what stakeholder interests need to be considered for long-term business and societal welfare.

Trends in Corporate Performance Measurement

Challenges to the international competitiveness of American firms helped to catapult TQM to prominence in the second half of the 1980s. Initially, the typical TQM focus was improvement of manufacturing processes, using techniques such as statistical process control, just-in-time inventory, and quality circles, to elicit innovative ideas from employees. From this TQM foundation, a number of paths emerged to further improve company processes; for example, the re-engineering path concentrated on efficiencies related to the critical processes driving success. But, for these change management programs to be effective, performance measurement systems needed change to reflect the new priorities (Lynch and Cross, 1991; Brancato, 1995).

A significant insight from this period was that traditional cost accounting systems failed to report on customer satisfaction, employee morale, the rate of innovation, etc., that contribute to long-term growth and financial success. The traditional accounting measures focused on simple financial data and only on past results (Johnson and Kaplan, 1987).

In the field of managerial accounting, Kaplan and Norton at Harvard Business School designed the "Balanced Scorecard": an approach to cost accounting focused on the collection and use of information critical to strategic planning and control. Four areas of performance were distinguished: traditional financial measures; customer-related measures; internal business efficiency measures; and measures of innovation and learning (Kaplan and Norton, 1992).

This effort triggered a wide array of commentary in academic circles, and interest in the business community (Kaplan and Norton, 1996a, b). In the early 1990s, for example, the United States Competitiveness Policy Council initiated a study of non-financial key performance measures (Brancato, 1995), and management consulting firms eagerly devised systems to improve performance measurement (e.g., Vitale and Mavrinac, 1995). The Conference Board released two research reports about the various ways that firms identify their particular non-financial performance measures (Brancato, 1995; Hexel, 1997).

Kaplan and Norton clearly articulated that the instrumental goal of the Balanced Scorecard is to create value for shareholders. They did not consider or use the stakeholder term. However, others in the accounting field noted the gaps in Kaplan and Norton's model. In an in-depth case study, Butler, Letza, and Neale (1997) emphasized the importance of linking scorecard categories to the company's mission statement. They also noted that employees and local communities contribute significantly to strategic performance in many companies, but were ignored in Balanced Scorecard categories.

Convergence on an Expanded View of Stakeholders?

An expanded definition of stakeholders and the impacts on them might be emerging in the accounting field. For example, Atkinson, Waterhouse, and Wells (1997) assert that the stakeholder concept is relevant to strategic performance measurement and note that senior managers can shape the nature and scope of stakeholder-firm relationships. They criticize the process approach of Kaplan and Norton's Balanced Scorecard for three reasons:

1. It does not emphasize the role of employees and suppliers on strategic performance.
2. It fails to identify the community's role in establishing the contextual environment for the company's activities.
3. It does not "identify performance measurement as a two-way process, which enables management to assess stakeholders' contributions to the company's primary and secondary goals and enables stakeholders to assess whether the organization is capable of fulfilling its obligations to them now and in the future" (Atkinson, Waterhouse, and Wells, 1997: 26).

A second example of recent quality improvement initiatives, developed by Arthur Andersen, is "Global Insights 98" (Arthur Andersen, 1997: S5). The theme is "Best Practices: Driving Growth through Innovation, Alliances and Stakeholder Symbiosis." In written descriptions of the initiative, the word "stakeholder" is not deemed to warrant explanation, but the word, "symbiosis" is:

> Symbiosis is not another word for balance. . . . Borrowing from the field of biology, symbiosis is an emerging practice that can move a company beyond the limitation of stakeholder balance to a mutuality that enables each to flourish in a system where all must flourish (Anonymous, 1997: S3).

Stakeholder symbiosis is touted as a win-win result. It is based on a model of abundance, rather than scarcity, so that each stakeholder is improved, but not at the expense of other stakeholders. This vision of stakeholder involvement appears compatible with the vision embedded in the business and society literature. Yet, the specific list of stakeholders in this initiative is underdeveloped, with only five given: employees, suppliers, customers, society, and shareholders (Arthur Andersen, 1997: S5). Apparently, the all-encompassing "society" stands for all the specific groups outside the traditional managerial view. Consider how much more effective this description would be if it named precisely the diverse groups embedded in "society," such as local communities, government, the media, and voluntary organizations. Their claims and interests, power, and legitimacy with respect to any particular business organization are often quite different from those of traditional stakeholders and from one another. Given the rising importance of stakeholders in management thinking and practice, this research project focuses on how companies integrate stakeholder awareness into their performance measurement processes.

Pilot Study Methodology and Findings

Seventeen firms headquartered in the southeastern United States completed the questionnaire: 35 percent from Georgia, 41 percent from North Carolina, and 24 percent from South Carolina. Annual sales for these companies range from $1.5 million to $500 million, with an average of $115 million. Survey questions asked about changes in internal data collection and reporting over the past five years; the extent to which stakeholder interests have been incorporated in internal/external reporting and, ultimately, strategic planning; and who receives reports of non-financial performance measures.

Currently, most of the pilot firms (59 percent) do not utilize a standard approach to non-financial performance measurement. The companies that use standard approaches named methods including: Balanced Scorecard, customized matrix profile, management by objectives assay, and performance ratios. However, most pilot study firms (81 percent) expect future changes in the performance measures used by their firms. Almost three-fifths (59 percent) expect that these measures will be disclosed more widely in the future, and that those disclosures will be mandated by external groups (56 percent). Examples of such groups included: government, Wall Street, the Financial Accounting Standards Board (FASB), the Securities and Exchange Commission (SEC), the Occupational Safety and Health Administration (OSHA), the Environmental Protection Agency (EPA), investors, lenders, and activist groups.

Non-financial performance measures identified in the literature are widely diverse, non-standardized, and not consistently quantified. We identified fourteen dimensions in the literature reported to be in use today (Brancato, 1995; Hexel, 1997):

1. Community Support/Approval
2. Customer Satisfaction/Retention
3. Employee Diversity
4. Employee Satisfaction/Retention
5. Employee Training
6. Environmental Competitiveness
7. Environmental Safety
8. Innovation
9. Internal Process Efficiencies
10. Market Growth
11. New Product Development
12. R&D Investments
13. R&D Productivity
14. Relations with Suppliers

We asked pilot firms four questions regarding these dimensions, whose results are reported here.

Q1: Which of the areas of performance does your company currently and routinely measure?

If a firm is what it measures, Table 1 results show that these firms are customer/employee/market driven. Half again as many companies report that they measure customer satisfaction as market growth and employee satisfaction, the second highest categories. Over half also measure performance in employee training. All other categories were reported to be routinely measured by less than half of the respondents. This suggests that these companies are applying the managerial view of stakeholder involvement, although supplier stakeholder relationships received little mention (29 percent).

Table 1:   Current Performance Measurement Practices

Dimension	% Routinely Measuring (n=17)
Customer Satisfaction/Retention	88
Market Growth	59
Employee Satisfaction/Retention	59
Employee Training	53
Internal Process Efficiencies	47
New Product Development	41
Environmental Safety	35
Relations with Suppliers	29
R&D Productivity	29
Employee Diversity	24
R&D Investments	24
Community Support/Approval	18
Innovation	18
Environmental Competitiveness	6

Q2: For each measurement used, which primary stakeholder group concerns (up to 3) are you responding to?

Table 2 lists the stakeholder groups for the top three performance measures reported in Q1. Customers predictably drive customer satisfaction/retention, but over half of those surveyed said they were also responding to their employees' interests. Employee satisfaction/retention is most directly related to the concerns of employees, of course, but these firms also report that the satisfaction and retention of employees is, to a lesser extent, relevant to customers. If customers are stakeholders associated with the well-being of employees, a link between happy and effective employees and customer satisfaction/retention is implied. Table 2 shows that monitoring of market growth is driven by responsiveness to stockholders and Wall Street firms, and also to employees in half of the respondent firms.

Table 2: Primary Stakeholders

Performance Measure	Primary Stakeholders	% Responsive to Primary Stakeholders (n=17)
Customer Satisfaction/Retention	Customers	100
	Employees	53
	Stockholders	40
Employee Satisfaction/Retention	Employees	100
	Customers	30
	Stockholders	20
Market Growth	Stockholders	90
	Wall Street	70
	Employees	50

Q3: To what extent does each performance measure link to strategic planning?

Table 3 reports the linkage between non-financial performance dimensions and the strategic planning process, in decreasing order of strength. For this question, the following scale was employed: 1 = no specific link, 2 = several weak links, 3 = several important links, 4 = many significant links, 5 = fully linked.

In general, companies that indicate high-priority interest in a measurement appear to link it to their strategic planning process. An interesting finding relates to employee satisfaction/retention whose relatively high mean score (2.82) is significantly lower than that of market growth (3.65). This difference suggests that, although an equal number of companies say they routinely measure employee satisfaction/retention and market growth, when performance measures are actually converted into strategy, market growth is given higher priority than employee satisfaction/retention.

Weakest among strategic links were relations with suppliers, R&D productivity, community support, and environmental competitiveness. Apparently the few firms (18 percent) in the pilot study that measure community support see it as only tangentially related to their long-term success. Even fewer measure, or are concerned strategically about, environmental competitiveness.

Table 3:   Performance Measure Links to Strategic Planning
            (n=17)

Dimension	Link	s.d.
Customer Satisfaction	3.88	1.22
Market Growth	3.65	1.84
New Product Development	2.94	1.76
Employee Satisfaction	2.82	1.74
Internal Process Efficiencies	2.76	1.75
Employee Training	2.47	1.50
Innovation	2.18	1.55
Environmental Safety	2.00	1.22
R&D Innovation	1.88	1.54
Relations with Suppliers	1.82	1.13
R&D Productivity	1.82	1.47
Community Support	1.53	1.07
Environmental Competitiveness	1.29	0.69

Q4: Who receives the measurements you routinely report?

Responses about recipients of routine non-financial performance measurement are summarized in Table 4.

Among the pilot firms, CEOs are most often the recipients of non-financial performance measure reports. Boards of directors receive about half as much information as the CEOs who report to them. Middle management is considerably better informed than the board on the performance of the firm. Wall Street, large investors, and other providers of capital are not generally supplied with internal performance reports.

Pilot survey results suggest that the majority of companies have begun to think about non-financial performance measures, but less than half have made progress in implementing specific new stakeholder-related approaches to performance measurement.

Case Study Methodology and Findings

The three companies (Amoco, PNC Bank, and Sears), identified as active in developing non-financial performance measurement systems, were interviewed intensively to learn more about their motivations, processes, and outcomes with respect to various stakeholders. These companies represent

Table 4: Recipients of Performance Measure Reports (n=17)

Recipient	Customer Satisfaction	Workplace Practices	Market Growth
CEO	80	88	90
Middle Management	67	63	60
Top Management Team	80	100	100
All Managers and Above	60	38	50
All Employees	47	38	40
Board of Directors	40	38	80
Selected Employees	40	26	30
Public Affairs Department	20		30
Large Investors	20	13	50
Wall Street Analysts	20	25	90
Other Providers of Capital	13	25	50
Industry Trade Associations	7	13	20
Community Groups	7		
Media	7		
Elected Officials	7		20
Labor Unions			10

diverse industries (i.e., petroleum/natural gas, banking, and retail sales) and diverse uses of non-traditional performance measures. Case reports for the companies, available from the authors, are summarized here.

Amoco

We interviewed three executives at Amoco's Chicago headquarters: two in the quality shared-services group and one in corporate training and development. The interviewees played distinct roles in setting up and maintaining Amoco's scorecard measurement process. While Amoco appears to have no exact equivalent to Kaplan and Norton's Balanced Scorecard, the company has devised scorecard measures reflecting its own view of the stakeholder environment and most important relationships. At Amoco, scorecarding is used primarily as an internal management tool, not as a way to impart performance information to external stakeholders.

The scorecarding process began in the mid-1990s when Amoco underwent a major restructuring to re-integrate management and operations. The Amoco Progress Measurement Team designed a three-phase process through which managers would learn about, and implement, the scorecard concept as a tool for performance evaluation. (The word "progress" equates to quality within Amoco.) Amoco's scorecards exist at three levels: strategic, business unit, and team.

Strategic scorecarding is defined as "an ongoing process of using strategic measurement to manage the business and improve performance over time. It includes a limited number of top-level measures that reflect the short- and long-term goals of the organization and the perspectives of key stakeholders" (Amoco, 1997). These measures relate to the Malcolm Baldrige Award criteria in six categories: customers, people, operations, product/service quality, suppliers, and financial and markets. The first phase in the three-phase process involves strategic alignment and leadership during which top managers develop a strategic template. This template guides the selection of design measures and performance targets in the second phase. In the third phase, the scorecard is implemented in business units and teams and then refined. By mid-1998, three Amoco groups had completed pilot implementation projects, and the strategic scorecarding process was ready to be fully deployed.

Business units and *teams* are encouraged to create their own measurement criteria, weights, and measurement indicators within overall Amoco parameters. This approach improves management support of the process and the value of using the tool. However, this bottom-up approach complicates the step of aggregating results at higher levels in the organization. About 80 percent of the criteria are similar across all scorecards, and relate to such organizational features as asset utilization, cost control, customer focus, and teamwork. About 20 percent of the criteria are unique to the units and teams; for example, one unit includes technology transfer among its assessment criteria. As with any measurement process, adding results across different types of functions presents a challenge.

The Progress group intended to roll out the strategic scorecarding process to the rest of the corporation over the following year. However, subsequent to our interviews, the proposed merger of Amoco with British Petroleum was announced. The merger may affect the implementation schedule and perhaps even the scorecarding process itself. Future interviews will provide an answer.

PNC Bank Corporation

We interviewed two executives in the Treasury Management Division (TMD) of Corporate Banking at PNC Bank: one is the director of Human Resources, who organized the Balanced Scorecard process in early 1998; the other works in a service department implementing the scorecard process for the first time. TMD is one of the first divisions in the bank to use the scorecard as a performance measurement tool.

TMD's categories were structured after Kaplan and Norton's original Balanced Scorecard. Short-term strategic objectives for the division were identified in brainstorming sessions, and the top fifteen were selected and assigned to one of the four quadrants (i.e., customers; financial; internal processes; and learning and growth). Each of the division's nine service departments was then allowed to specify its own three goals, which were placed in the appropriate quadrant. Targets were established for each objective, including a minimum threshold and an "exceeding target" value. The financial department is responsible for producing quarterly reports of scorecard results, which are reported to the CEO and Board of Directors and summarized in the division's newsletter. Incentive pay is tied to scorecard results.

Initial implementation of the Scorecard resulted in several challenges: information overload for employees; employee cynicism about future uses of the tool; need for improved measures; and need to shift to a long-term strategic focus. TMD plans to address the linkage to long-term objectives within the overall organizational mission in the next cycle. A beneficial outcome of Balanced Scorecard implementation was the identification of critical management skills that require training and development.

Sears

We interviewed an executive-level vice president for organizational transformation. Sears has the most thoroughly integrated and mature scorecard implementation among the case study organizations. Since 1993, when poor financial performance resulted in a change in top leadership, the company has worked through an organizational change process that uses non-traditional performance measurement.

The new CEO convened a corporate visioning conference for top management in 1993, and later, non-financial performance measurement was logically related to the new Sears vision, values, and objectives that emerged. Transformation of the organization required effective communication with 321,000 associates, accomplished by using innovative "learning maps" and "town hall" meetings. The learning maps provide a graphical picture of a physical environment (e.g., a river) to portray relationships among significant variables. By early 1998, every associate had been exposed to three different learning maps in small group sessions. Larger groups of employees attended local town hall meetings and brainstormed about how to achieve the strategic objectives related to the learning map themes.

Sears developed a performance assessment model for data collection and analysis called "Total Performance Indicators" (TPI). This set of measures relates to three stakeholder groups (employees, customers, and investors) and demonstrates the significant predictive power of the employee-customer-profit chain. Key indicator data are reported not only to top management but also are regularly made available to every associate through a corporate database. Almost all managers have some compensation tied to non-financial performance measures.

Sears plans to continue to use non-traditional performance measurement for strategic planning and implementation. The TPI model is being tailored to the individual associate level in novel ways. For example, sales associates get feedback on specific customer transactions via telephone surveys randomly administered in real-time. Executives plan for all associates to have some pay incentives linked to non-financial performance, eventually.

Observations from Case Studies

Common elements emerged from the initial set of case study interviews:

- Significant triggering events cause companies to recognize the need for more comprehensive performance systems that link internal structures and processes to more demanding external pressures. Employee behaviors need to be more tightly coordinated to higher-level strategic objectives.
- No consistent measures or reporting methods are yet emerging across companies. Instead, each company fits certain common features, such as measurement of customer satisfaction, into its existing management system.

Amoco's scorecarding process has several interesting features, among which are:

- A business unit's "customers" are not necessarily external stakeholders, but may be other Amoco business units with whom joint project work is performed. This recognition of within-company units as customers is an unexplored topic in stakeholder theory that is worth research attention.
- Amoco has an 80/20 split between common elements and unique elements in the business unit and team scorecards. This split is compatible with the general theory of corporate social performance, which allows for commonalities across businesses, operating units, and individual teams, but also emphasizes the importance of identifying specific configurations of stakeholder impacts, task responsibilities, etc. Context-specific measurement practices are necessary to capture performance in meaningful ways.

The specific application of Kaplan and Norton's Balanced Scorecard process and categories in PNC's TM Division is a unique experiment that is likely to have significant impacts on the future form of non-financial performance measurement throughout the organization. Tracking how shortcuts taken in the first application of the tool are dealt with in the second cycle (especially the expansion from short-term to longer-term objectives), is important.

Sears has pioneered the precise measurement of quantitative relationships between employee morale, customer satisfaction, and profitability. The use of learning maps to communicate these relationships to a large workforce is considered critical to the transformation of Sears. The company's TPI model is potentially revolutionary in replacing the stockholder-only orientation with a broader employee-customer-stockholder perspective across American corporations.

Implications and Next Steps

This research project examines the question of how stakeholder interests and pressures impact corporate performance measurement and reporting. This is a good time to look at corporate performance measurement because a number of companies have expanded their internal performance reporting to include measures beyond traditional monthly or quarterly financial data in the calculation of cash flows and payback periods. However, despite their perceptions that reporting of more non-financial data will be required in the future, the majority of firms in the pilot study are not proactively designing their own key performance measurement systems. For those that are using non-financial data in performance measurement, results show little evidence that they employ a broad definition of stakeholders. Rather, these firms typically reflect a shift from the stockholder-only model to the traditional managerial model in which customers and employees are also considered important stakeholders.

Companies interviewed in the second phase of the research project are developing their own approaches to non-financial performance measurement, but each is clearly immersed in the traditional managerial model where the interests of employees, customers, and shareholders are each important. Some movement toward an expanded view of stakeholders is suggested at Amoco where individual teams identify the "customers" for their work, which may include government agencies and other partners. Sears may add more stakeholders to its model. PNC Bank is still learning about how non-financial performance measures can be used effectively. A second round of interviews is needed to track the experiences of these firms in applying and learning from stakeholder-oriented performance measures.

The contribution of this exploratory research is an initial analysis of the extent to which stakeholders have actually affected corporate internal performance measurement practices, and of the differential impacts of various stakeholder groups. Creative approaches to incorporating an expanded view of stakeholders should be emphasized and publicized. The study's findings should help executives to consider stakeholder theory when designing non-financial performance measures and may contribute to refining stakeholder theory itself.

Jeanne M. Logsdon *(jlogsdon@unm.edu)* is a professor in the Organizational Studies Department at the Robert O. Anderson Schools of Management, University of New Mexico, Albuquerque, NM 87131-1221.

Patsy Granger Lewellyn *(lewelln@vm.sc.edu)* is a professor of accounting and management information systems at the School of Business Administration, University of South Carolina at Aiken, SC 29801.

References

Amoco. [c.1997]. *Amoco strategic scorecarding process: Measurement and assessment.* [Company brochure, undated.]

Anonymous. 1997. Best practices for global competitiveness: Driving growth through innovation, alliances and stakeholder symbiosis. *Business Week*, Sept.: S1-S30. ["Special Advertising Section" from a Sept. issue.]

Arthur Andersen. 1997. Overview: Global Insights 98, Discovery Tool [survey]. In: Best practices for global competitiveness: Driving growth through innovation, alliances and stakeholder symbiosis. *Business Week*, Sept.: S1-S30. ["Special Advertising Section" from a Sept. issue.]

Atkinson, A.A., Waterhouse, J.H., and Wells, R.B. 1997. A stakeholder approach to strategic performance measurement. *Sloan Management Review*, 38 (3): 25-37.

Brancato, C. 1995. *New corporate performance measures: A research report.* Report no. 1118-95-RR. New York: Conference Board.

Butler, A., Letza, S., and Neale, B. 1997. Linking the balanced scorecard to strategy. *Long Range Planning*, 30 (2): 242-53.

Carroll, A. 1996. *Business and society: Ethics and stakeholder management.* 3rd ed. Cincinnati: South-Western College Publishing.

Clarkson, M.B.E., ed. 1998. *The corporation and its stakeholders: Classic and contemporary readings.* Toronto: University of Toronto Press.

Donaldson, T., and Preston, L.E. 1995. The stakeholder theory of the corporation: Concepts, evidence, and implications. *Academy of Management Review*, 20 (1): 65-91.

Freeman, R.E. 1984. *Strategic management: A stakeholder approach.* Boston: Pitman.

Harrison, J., and St. John, C. 1996. Managing and partnering with external stakeholders. *Academy of Management Executive*, 10 (2): 46-60.

Hexel, E., ed. 1997. *Case studies in strategic performance measurement.* Report no. 1176-97-CR. New York: Conference Board.

Johnson, H., and Kaplan, R. 1987. *Relevance lost–The rise and fall of management accounting.* Boston: Harvard Business School Press.

Jones, T.M., ed. 1994. The Toronto conference: Reflections on stakeholder theory. *Business & Society*, 33 (1): 82-131. [Special section.]

Jones, T. 1995. Instrumental stakeholder theory: A synthesis of ethics and economics. *Academy of Management Review*, 20 (2): 404-437.

Kaplan, R., and Norton, D. 1992. The balanced scorecard–Measures that drive performance. *Harvard Business Review*, 70 (Jan.-Feb.): 71-79.

Kaplan, R., and Norton, D. 1996a. Using the balanced scorecard as a strategic management system. *Harvard Business Review*, 74 (Jan.-Feb.): 75-85.

Kaplan, R., and Norton, D. 1996b. Linking the balanced scorecard to strategy. *California Management Review*, 39 (1): 53-79.

Kotter, J., and Heskett, J. 1992. *Corporate culture and performance*. New York: Free Press.

Lynch, R., and Cross, K. 1991. *Measure up! Yardsticks for continuous improvement*. Cambridge, MA: Blackwell.

Mitchell, R.K., Agle, B.R., and Wood, D.J. 1997. Toward a theory of stakeholder identification and salience: Defining the principle of who and what really counts. *Academy of Management Review*, 22 (4): 853-886.

Nàsi, J., ed. 1995. *Understanding stakeholder thinking*. Helsinki: LSR Publications.

Vitale, M., and Mavrinac, S. 1995. How effective is your performance measurement system? *Management Accounting* (New York), 77 (2) (Aug.): 43-47.

Windsor, D. 1992. Stakeholder management in multinational enterprises. In *Proceedings of the Third Annual Meeting of the International Association for Business and Society held in Leuven, Belgium, 13-20 June 1992*, ed. S. Brenner and S. Waddock: 121-127.

Company Reactions to Socially Responsible Investing: An Empirical Analysis

Harry J. Van Buren III, University of Pittsburgh
Karen Paul, Florida International University

Introduction

The present study, exploratory in nature, seeks to understand how corporate executives perceive socially responsible investment (SRI) organizations, and how they react to public scrutiny of their corporation's social performance. After briefly describing the SRI movement, and socially responsible investors as stakeholders, we discuss the results of our empirical study in which corporate secretaries and investor relations officials responded to questions about SRI. We conclude that while corporations still lack familiarity with the SRI movement, SRI groups do have some influence on corporations. Further, and not surprisingly, corporate officers disagree with the goals (expressed in terms of legitimacy) of SRI actors. Finally, results demonstrate that the broader concerns of shareholder activists and allied research organizations are taken seriously, and that legal counsel and senior management may be most likely to formulate a response to the issues they raise.

Background: The SRI Movement

In all of its forms, socially responsible investing (SRI) has increased dramatically in recent years. It connects investment decisions to social concerns in three ways to be discussed here: screening portfolios on the basis of social criteria, filing shareholder resolutions, and creating information about corporate social performance (CSP).

Portfolio Screening

The use of ethical criteria for investment decision making is not new. Seventeenth-century Quakers, for example, refused to profit from war or from the slave trade (Kinder, Lydenberg, and Domini, 1993). The South African anti-apartheid movement is marked as the traditional start of modern shareholder activism and SRI (Kinder, Lydenberg, and Domini, 1993; Massie, 1998), because it led to the exclusion in portfolios of companies with South African involvement. South Africa's all-race election in 1994 did not bring about the death of SRI, as some observers had predicted. Instead, individual and institutional investors developed other "social screens" reflective of their values as criteria by which to judge companies for portfolio inclusion/exclusion. The United States-based Interfaith Center on Corporate Responsibility (ICCR) examines, on behalf of religious institutional investors, for example, corporate social responsibility in areas including environmental responsibility, international human rights, equal employment opportunity, board diversity, and the use of images of Native Americans in advertising (Van Buren, 1995).

Shareholder Resolutions

Two brothers, John and Lewis Gilbert, may have been the first American shareholder activists. In the 1930s they raised corporate governance issues at thousands of corporate annual meetings (Marx, 1992). Since then, shareholder activists, especially over the last quarter century, have used the resolution process, outlined in Rule 14(a)(8) of the U.S. Securities and Exchange Act of 1934, to bring about social change by influencing managers. By this process, individuals or institutions (proponents) meeting certain minimum ownership requirements can submit a shareholder resolution (e.g., to adopt particular policies) for inclusion on a corporation's proxy statement. If the proponents and the company do not come to an agreement, the resolution is considered by shareholders at the company's annual meeting (Van Buren, 1995). Although most shareholder resolutions fail to receive a majority of shareholder votes, they are an invaluable tool of activist groups because they are a low-cost means of bringing public attention to issues (Zampa and McCormick, 1991), and often provide proponents with direct access to corporate executives. Increasingly, endowments, public pension funds, and unions have used the shareholder resolution process to press their interests in order to influence corporate behavior.

CSP Information

Shareholder activists consistently make two points: that moral minimums exist for all corporate activities, and that more information about these activities and corporate social performance (CSP) is better than less. In response, SRI-focused research groups that produce CSP information have emerged in increasing numbers. The American-based company, Kinder, Lydenberg, and Domini (KLD), for example, creator of the Socrates database of CSP profiles (see Waddock and Graves, 1997 for a description of profiles as proxies for CSP), analyzes the actions of companies in social performance terms and provides reports to interested investors. Other groups, such as the Council on Economic Priorities (CEP), report to members on the social and environmental records of companies, and the Investor Responsibility Research Center (IRRC) publishes reports on social issue resolutions, describing the issues and the viewpoints held by companies and proponents. Groups like

KLD, the CEP, and IRRC might also be said to play an indirect activist role by uncovering information about corporate social performance. Once information is public, activists may have the information needed to influence change and companies the impetus to change their behavior to protect reputation or image. Although the amount of social performance information available now would have been unimaginable even ten years ago, it is still not as widely available as information about financial performance.

By any objective measure, the SRI movement has changed the behavior of many investors. There has been tremendous growth in the number of portfolios invested, at least in part, on the basis of social criteria, and many investors now include non-pecuniary considerations in their decision-making. ICCR members alone have more than $90 billion in investments (ICCR, 1997). Estimates of the total amount invested with some sort of social screen range up to $1 trillion. Whether SRI in any of its forms has affected managerial behavior, however, is less clear.

The present study seeks to understand corporate attitudes towards those organizations that engage in SRI, and how managers react when the corporate social performance records of their corporations are challenged: either directly (by shareholder resolution) or indirectly (when information about corporate social performance becomes public).

Socially Responsible Investors as Stakeholders

Because the Redefining the Corporation project focuses on stakeholders, answers are needed on how (and if) socially responsible investors, and research groups providing information on CSP, are in fact stakeholders. The classic definition of stakeholder–anyone who can affect or is affected by the achievement of the firm's objectives (Freeman, 1984)–offers a good starting point. Under this definition, as Mitchell, Agle and Wood (1997) note, almost anyone or anything (the environment, for example [Starik, 1995]) might be counted as a stakeholder. Certainly it is well recognized that shareholders, by virtue of their ownership stake, have at least some power over the firm's managers, making them stakeholders (but see Berle and Means, 1932 for a contrary view). But why and how particular stakeholders might affect managerial decision-making–because this is a stated objective, after all, of many shareholder activists and socially responsible investors–are the more relevant questions for the present study.

While a firm has many stakeholders, not all of them are interested in its corporate social performance. Socially responsible investors and social research firms, therefore, may play the role of self-designated monitors of corporate social performance, and so might be important in bringing more attention to a corporation's social behavior. Prior to Freeman's (1984) seminal work, Freeman and Reed (1983) discussed the stakeholder concept in terms of corporate governance. Using their reasoning, socially responsible investors proclaiming (and seeking to enforce) values contrary to those espoused by managers are attempting to participate in the governance of the organization. Wood and Jones (1995: 231) propose that stakeholders play at least three roles with respect to corporate social performance:

1. Stakeholders are the source of expectations about what constitutes desirable and undesirable firm performance.
2. Stakeholders experience the effects of corporate behavior; that is, they are the recipients of corporate actions and output.
3. Stakeholders evaluate how well firms have met expectations and/ or how firms' behaviors have affected the groups and organizations in their environment.

For socially responsible investors, points 1 and 3 might be most salient, because they are, and have been, an important source of expectations about CSP. Many of the issues identified by these investors (e.g., South African involvement and board diversity) have come into the public consciousness because of their efforts. Further, socially responsible investors' CSP evaluations may influence the decisions of some other investors; for example, those who would not research issues themselves may act on information once it is available. Whether they influence the behaviors of managers is the central question of this paper. As Lydenberg and Paul (1997: 213) note, socially responsible investors aim to create and support a business environment in which managers:

1. are mindful of the risks their operations impose on society.
2. avoid incalculable risks.
3. in the case of calculable risks, minimize social costs, are as equitable as possible in distributing social costs, and compensate fairly for any risks imposed.

Another way of looking at the issue of socially responsible investors as stakeholders is through the tripartite classification scheme of Mitchell, Agle and Wood (1997: 854). They propose that three relationship attributes–power to influence the firm, legitimacy of their relationship with the firm, and urgency of the stakeholder's claim on the firm–can define the salience of a stakeholder to an organization. These three attributes and their relevance to socially responsible investors are provided in Table 1.

Socially responsible shareholders will have influence over organizational managers to the degree that they possess power and/or legitimacy and/or urgency. If socially responsible investors lack one or more of these attributes, then their ability to influence organizational managers will be correspondingly limited. In the next section, we discuss the methods used in our empirical investigation that explore:

1. Managerial attitudes toward socially responsible investors.
2. Perceptions of the power, legitimacy, and urgency of those investors.
3. Corporate responses to negative CSP information.

Table 1:   *Stakeholder Relationship Attributes and Their Relevance to the Study of Socially Responsible Investor Influence over Organizational Managers*

Attribute	Description	Relevance to study of SRI
Power	The extent to which a access to coercive, utilitarian, or normative means of imposing its will on a relationship.	Socially responsible investors can seek to have their policies adopted by a corporation through the proxy process. More likely as a source of power, however, are normative means.
Legitimacy	A generalized perception that the actions of an entity are desirable, proper, or appropriate within some socially constructed system of norms, values, beliefs, and definitions (from Suchman, 1995).	To the degree that socially responsible investors are seen as legitimate, they will be able to have influence on managerial decision-making.
Urgency	The degree to which stakeholder claims call for immediate attention.	Socially responsible investors with claims perceived to be urgent (for example, those addressing issues of great public concern) are likely to get managerial attention.

Research Methods

Sample

A random sample of 225 companies was selected from the KLD Socrates database, which contains CSP information, collected by KLD, on approximately 650 companies.

We decided that two groups of corporate organizational members would receive mailed surveys. The first group consists of corporate secretaries who handle matters related to the proxy and resolution process and often coordinate dialogue between managers and shareholder proponents. Usable responses were received from only nineteen of 225 companies (8.4 percent), making the response rate too low for statistical analysis. A low response rate was expected due to the length of the survey and the population sampled.

A better response rate was attained for the second corporate sample. Questionnaires were sent to investor relations managers in the companies sampled, selected because of their role as the interface between the corporation and shareholders. Forty-eight usable responses (21.3 percent) gave a response rate for this group in line with that of previous studies of similar populations (Ruf, Muralidhar and Paul, 1993).

For comparative purposes, a smaller version of the questionnaire was sent to all of the members (150) of the ICCR governing board. From this cohort, fifty-six replies were received, yielding a response rate of 37.3 percent.

Measures

Because of the exploratory nature of this project, we decided to gather a significant amount of attitudinal data using a questionnaire. The first set of questions related to the respondent's awareness and perceptions of the importance and credibility of a number of the organizations associated with SRI (Table 2). Other organizations (e.g., the Conference Board) were included in lists for comparative purposes. Respondents were asked to rate each organization on five-point Likert scales, anchored by Not at all aware/ Highly aware; Not at all important/ Highly important; Not at all credible/ Highly credible.

Table 2: *Organizations Involved in Socially Responsible Investment and Other Organizations Named in the Questionnaire*

Name	Description
CalPERS	California state employees' pension fund; involved in activism on corporate governance issues.
Council on Economic Priorities	Provides information about CSP.
Interfaith Center on Corporate Responsibility	Clearinghouse of religious institutional investors involved in shareholder activism.
Investor Responsibility Research Center	Tracks social issue shareholder resolutions and provides some information about CSP.
Kinder, Lydenberg, and Domini	Provides information about CSP.
Other organizations (included for comparative purposes):	
Business Roundtable	Advocacy organization for the business community.
Conference Board	Advocacy organization for the business community; also conducts research.
Council of Institutional Investors	Membership organization of institutional investors, most of whom are not engaged in SRI.
National Association of Manufacturers	Advocacy organization for manufacturers.
Council on Scientific Management	"Dummy" organization.

The second set of questions related to the stakeholder relationship attributes of power, legitimacy, and urgency identified by Mitchell, Agle and Wood (1997). We recast "power" in terms of "influence" because, while most shareholders have little direct power over managers (see Berle and Means, 1932; Kaufman, Zacharias, and Karson, 1995), they may be able to exercise influence. Legitimacy and urgency were used as defined in Table 1. These questions used five-point Likert scales anchored by No influence/ Significant influence; Completely illegitimate/ Highly legitimate; Not at all urgent/ Extremely urgent.

Corporate respondents were then asked how they would respond to negative news about their organization's social performance. They were asked to indicate how likely it was that they would discuss this information with the following organizational members: corporate counsel, human resources, investor relations, members of the board, outside consultants, and senior management. Respondents were asked to name the three individuals/groups who would play the most critical roles in formulating a response to the negative social information.

Next, corporate respondents were asked about their awareness of, and the effect of, shareholder criticism on issues raised by socially responsible investors: board diversity, corporate governance, equal employment opportunity in the United States, environmental responsibility, executive compensation, human rights standards, vendor standards, wage levels for foreign employees, and the use of images of Native Americans in advertising. (ICCR members were asked only about their awareness.) All of these issues had been the subject of shareholder resolutions in the past year (ICCR, 1998), and have been of concern historically to socially responsible investors.

The corporate questionnaire concluded with a question about the social issue that received the most attention from the company in the previous year. Respondents were asked to identify the issue, indicate who developed corporate policy on the issue, and describe the result. Both the corporate and ICCR questionnaires requested demographic information about the respondent's organization.

Anonymity was promised to respondents, although the questionnaires were coded for follow-up efforts. The next section describes some of our results, focusing most particularly on issues related to attitudes, awareness, and perceptions of stakeholder relationship attributes possessed by socially responsible investors.

Results

Comparisons between the groups in this study should be undertaken with great care because of the low response rate for the corporate secretary group. Even so, we think that the data from the questionnaires provides some interesting insights for the formulation of stakeholder theory.

Awareness, Perceived Importance, and Credibility

Results for each of the three groups of respondents–corporate secretaries, investor relations directors (corporate respondents), and ICCR governing board members–on their awareness of, perceived importance of, and perceived credibility of the organizations listed in Table 2, are as follows:

On all three measures, SRI groups (e.g., ICCR, KLD, and CEP) received lower scores from corporate respondents than from ICCR governing board members; these groups were also rated lower than industry-related groups (with the exception of CalPERS).

Further, investor relations personnel–whose position in the company puts them in contact with shareholders to a greater extent than corporate secretaries–generally rated SRI groups higher on all three dimensions. Tentatively, we conclude that there is not widespread awareness of the organizations that make up the SRI movement, and the perceived credibility of such groups among corporate personnel is quite low.

Stakeholder Relationship Attributes: Power, Legitimacy, and Urgency

Recall the role that the relationship attributes–power, legitimacy, and urgency–play in stakeholder salience: the level of stakeholder influence on corporate managers depends on the degree to which the stakeholder possesses any or all of these attributes. Based on corporate respondents' perception of these attributes, non-SRI groups generally received higher ratings on all three dimensions than SRI groups. Based on our results, we tentatively conclude that the general stakeholder salience of SRI groups is fairly low.

On all three dimensions, corporate respondents rated SRI groups negatively, again, with investor relations personnel giving somewhat higher ratings. As in the previous section of this data, CalPERS was rated more highly on all three dimensions.

These results would probably be troubling to SRI groups (e.g., ICCR and CEP), but it is not surprising that their perceived legitimacy would be low-rated by corporate respondents. That SRI groups' urgency rating is low *is* surprising, given that such groups believe themselves to be raising urgent issues with managers. We tentatively conclude that the stakeholder salience of SRI groups for most companies at most points in time is quite low. In any case, their perceived legitimacy will generally be low, as well. Socially responsible investors, by virtue of the issues they raise and the actions they ask corporate managers to take, will likely always be seen as less-than-completely "legitimate" by managers.

Specific Corporate Responsibility Issues

We queried both ICCR and corporate respondents about their awareness of social activism and criticism of companies around specific issues (e.g., board diversity, etc.). Corporate respondents were also asked to assess the influence of social activism on these issues on their company.

Results indicated that awareness of corporate respondents about specific issues raised by social critics was quite high for most issues. Awareness levels were similar to, though slightly lower than, those of ICCR respondents. Over time, therefore, the issues raised by socially responsible investors have at least gained the notice of organizational managers. Further, awareness is higher for issues that have been of concern to such investors for many years (e.g., board diversity, equal employment opportunity, and environmental responsibility) than for more recent issues (e.g., vendor standards and the use of images of Native Americans in advertising). Socially responsible investors and shareholder activists have not been the only groups raising these issues, but results show that their activities have had an impact on corporate managers, at least in raising awareness of different points of view.

On the five-point scale, ratings of the degree of influence of social activists on the issues were lower than the awareness ratings of issues. As with awareness, investors relations managers rated the influence of social activism more highly than corporate secretaries, and perceived influence was lower for newer issues.

Discussing Negative Social Information about the Corporation
Finally, we were interested in the processes by which corporations respond to negative social information. One way in which a stakeholder might gain salience is by creating and disseminating negative social information about a corporation's policies and practices. Such information might, for example, decrease the corporation's public legitimacy and demand some sort of corporate response. Certainly, both shareholder activists (by filing resolutions) and social research firms (by assessing and rating CSP) help make public negative CSP information.

Corporate respondents were asked to indicate with whom they would discuss the negative information about their corporation's social record and to name the three groups/individuals who would most likely formulate a response to the negative social information. The role that corporate counsel was reported to have played as a recipient of negative social information suggests that many companies take a legal approach to handling negative news about CSP. Not only was it likely that corporate counsel would be contacted, but more than half of the respondents in each group (75 percent of investor relations managers and 76 percent of corporate secretaries) indicated that corporate counsel was among the three groups/individuals that would play a critical role in formulating a response to negative social information about their company. For both corporate secretaries and investor relations personnel, the three groups are senior management, corporate counsel, and investor relations.

Results show that members of the board play a relatively unimportant role in responding to negative social information. Given that many shareholder resolutions ask boards of directors to undertake studies or to create policies thought to improve CSP, it is somewhat surprising that board members would be rated as less critical than others in the organization. (Fourteen percent of investor relations managers and 15 percent of corporate secretaries listed members of the board as one of the three critical individuals/ groups that would formulate a response to negative social information.) This finding suggests that companies may respond to negative social information in ways that are unconnected to long-term policy formulation, because that function is associated with most boards of directors.

Discussion, Future Directions, and Conclusions

In general, the SRI movement, while having some influence, is still seen by corporate managers as espousing "illegitimate" goals. Even when we cast power in terms of influence (following the stakeholder model of Mitchell, Agle and Wood, 1997), groups like ICCR and CEP are not thought to be influential or particularly salient by corporate managers. However, concerns about corporate governance do seem to receive greater respect from managers (likely because of higher proxy votes for shareholder resolutions addressing corporate governance issues than social issues). Because CalPERS has played a leading role in debates about corporate governance policies and has backed up its advocacy with organizational resources, it is seen as more influential than these other organizations. Moreover, because the values that CalPERS represents–principally, better corporate governance–are widely shared by the business community, it is seen as a more legitimate and, therefore, more salient stakeholder than social issue activists, for example, religious groups asking companies to ensure that a living wage is paid to their suppliers' or subcontractors' employees.

Stakeholder salience–at least in the SRI area–depends in part on managerial agreement with a stakeholder's goals. Because religious institutional investors and social research firms espouse values and goals not widely shared by corporate managers, these stakeholder groups are seen as less salient (and especially less legitimate) than organizations such as CalPERS. Given that most social issue shareholder resolutions receive support from shareholders in single-digit percentages, the low rating of the influence of SRI groups is not surprising. This said, there is widespread awareness of many of the CSP-related issues raised by such investors. If, then, one is looking for a way to express the influence of the SRI movement, it is in terms of advancing issues germane to CSP assessments that then become part of the public discourse, even if managers disagree with the values so expressed. We can say with some confidence that the SRI movement has helped to create and to support a business environment in which managers are mindful of the risks and costs their operations impose on society (Lydenberg and Paul, 1997), but the influence of the movement is small when compared to the values and norms of business.

Finally, we provide a glimpse of the ways in which corporate managers respond to negative news about their corporation's social performance. The involvement of corporate counsel, senior management, and investor relations officials indicates that responses to negative information about corporate social performance tend to focus on legal and public relations concerns. The board of directors, which is charged with representing the interests of shareholders, is less involved in formulating a response and may not even hear the negative information that comes to the attention of managers.

We conclude that the SRI movement has affected the public debate in terms of what good CSP looks like, but that its members are not seen by managers as legitimate, salient stakeholders. The accomplishments of the SRI movement are real and noteworthy, however. Anecdotal evidence suggests (even though empirical evidence is slight) that socially responsible investors played an important role in the anti-apartheid coalition, and today help bring to light issues like equal employment opportunity, environmental responsibility, wage levels of foreign workers, and others. We do not yet know how such investors influence managerial behavior and how this influence occurs. The present study has been one small step in enhancing our understanding of these issues, but further work is needed.

Understanding the influence of outsiders on corporate managers is difficult because many of the decision-making processes of organizations are hidden from public view. But it is precisely these internal processes–developing responses to stakeholders who are making social and ethical demands on companies–that are of greatest interest to researchers of stakeholder theory. Groups like religious institutional investors seemingly have little direct power and yet are able to exercise at least some influence. Unpacking how (and if) dissident stakeholders affect managerial decision-making and behavior is, therefore, one step toward a better stakeholder theory of the firm. If one is looking for a group of such stakeholders to study, socially responsible investors are good candidates.

Harry J. Van Buren III (*HarryVB@aol.com*) is completing Ph.D. research at the Joseph M. Katz Graduate School of Business, University of Pittsburgh, Pittsburgh, PA 15260, and is currently Assistant Professor of Business at Roberts Wesleyan College in Rochester, NY.

Karen Paul (*paulk@fiu.edu*) is Professor and Associate Dean at the College of Business Administration, Florida International University, 11200 Southwest

8th Street, Miami, FL 33199.

References

Berle, A.A., and Means, G.C. 1932. *The modern corporation and private property*. New York: Macmillan.

Freeman, R.E. 1984. *Strategic management: A stakeholder approach*. Boston: Pitman.

Freeman, R.E., and Evan, W.M. 1990. Corporate governance: A stakeholder perspective. *Journal of Behavioral Economics*, 19 (4): 337-359.

Freeman, R.E., and Reed, D.L. 1983. Stockholders and stakeholders: A new perspective on corporate governance. *California Management Review*, 25 (3): 83-94.

Interfaith Center on Corporate Responsibility. 1997. *1997 ICCR annual report*. New York: ICCR.

———. 1998. *1998 Proxy book*.

Kaufman, A., Zacharias, L., and Karson, M. 1995. *Managers vs. owners: The struggle for corporate control in American democracy*. New York: Oxford University Press.

Kinder, P., Lydenberg, S.D., and Domini, A.L. 1993. *Investing for good: Making money while being socially responsible*. New York: Harper Business.

Lydenberg, S.D., and Paul, K. 1997. Stakeholder theory and socially responsible investing: Toward a convergence of theory and practice. In *Proceedings of the Eighth Annual Meeting of the International Association for Business and Society held in Destin, FL, 6-9 March 1997*, ed. J. Weber and K. Rehbein: 208-213.

Marx, T.G. 1992. Corporate social performance reporting. *Public Relations Quarterly*, 37 (Winter 1992/1993): 38-44.

Massie, R.K. 1998. *Loosing the bonds: The United States and South Africa in the post-apartheid years*. New York: Doubleday.

Mitchell, R.K., Agle, B.R., and Wood, D.J. 1997. Toward a theory of stakeholder identification and salience: Defining the principle of who and what really counts. *Academy of Management Review*, 22 (4): 853-886.

Ruf, B., Muralidhar, K., and Paul, K. 1993. Eight dimensions of corporate social performance: Determination of relative importance using the analytic hierarchy process. In *Academy of Management Best Papers Proceedings 1993, 53rd Annual Meeting, Atlanta, GA, 8-11 August, 1993*, ed. D.P. Moore: 326-330.

Starik, M. 1995. Should trees have managerial standing? Toward stakeholder status for non-human nature. *Journal of Business Ethics*, 14 (3): 207-213.

Suchman, M.C. 1995. Managing legitimacy: Strategic and institutional approaches. *Academy of Management Review*, 20 (3) (July): 571-610.

Van Buren III, H.J. 1995. Business ethics for the new millennium. *Business and Society Review*, 93 (Spring): 51-55.

Waddock, S.A., and Graves, S.B. 1997. The corporate social performance-financial performance link. *Strategic Management Journal*, 18 (4): 303-319.

Wood, D.J., and Jones, R.E. 1995. Stakeholder mismatching: A theoretical problem in empirical research on corporate social performance. *International Journal of Organizational Analysis*, 3 (3): 229-267.

Zampa, F.P., and McCormick Jr., A.E. 1991. "Proxy power" and corporate democracy: The characteristics and efficacy of stockholder-initiated issues. *American Journal of Economics and Sociology*, 50 (1) (Jan.): 1-15.

Part 4

Conclusion

Redefining the Corporation: The Performance Link[1]

Jeanne M. Logsdon, University of New Mexico
Donna J. Wood, University of Pittsburgh

The Sloan grant to support and expand the development of the stakeholder concept is focused on the gaps between traditional views of management, which are embodied in neoclassical economic theory and contemporary finance theory, and new conceptualizations of management's roles and responsibilities. The field of business and society played an important role in championing the stakeholder concept in the 1980s and now has a significant opportunity to further influence the development of a stakeholder-based theory of the firm and society.

The stakeholder concept has clearly made headway in various business academic disciplines. But the actual content of these new uses of the term does not necessarily reflect our field's view of the meaning and value of "stakeholder." A recent article in *Sloan Management Review* provides a good example of what we mean by this statement. The article, "A Stakeholder Approach to Strategic Performance Measurement," promises:

> A model for measuring a company's performance helps all members–customers, suppliers, employees, and community–understand and evaluate their contributions and expectations. By focusing on the secondary processes for achieving primary objectives, such as profit, the system provides a tool for monitoring implicit and explicit contractual relationships with stakeholders (Atkinson, Waterhouse, and Wells, 1997: 25).

What's wrong with this view? Nothing is wrong with it as far as it goes; it is simply inadequate for the task. It is not really a new perspective at all, nor is it an accurate rendition of stakeholder theory. Instead it is but the traditional view of management financial responsibilities wrapped in stakeholder language. The only way to influence the firm in this view is through contracts, buying decisions, or litigation. And, since stakeholders in this view appear to be only those directly involved in profit achievement, a great many other interests and contributions are overlooked–particularly those with moral claims to be free from harm. Our view is that the stakeholder perspective, if it is to make any contribution to changing the neo-classical economic view of the firm and business-society relations, must be a more balanced view, examining various "primary objectives," including profitability, customer safety and satisfaction, employee safety and professional development, protection of the natural environment, and so on.

Furthermore, so-called primary and secondary objectives are too intertwined to be arranged in such a hierarchy. The idea of primary objectives is based in the first place on a Durkheimian notion of institutional division of labor, which was never meant to be so rigid that no crossovers were permitted. Scholars don't want to trivialize primary moral obligations, and this is just what can happen when their theories assume that profit is primary and all else is secondary. For example, the dolphins-and-tuna controversy of recent years was based on the moral problem of slaughtering one species in order to obtain another's commercial value. Who can speak for these animals? They are neither customers, suppliers, employees, nor community, yet their lives are lost and their species threatened with extinction because of corporate actions. Moral duties don't end because a victim is voiceless. After all, the dolphins can't stop buying tuna!

The distinctive competence offered by business and society researchers is not that we can develop or apply the finance model better than the finance academics can. Rather, it is that we see and are concerned with the rights and claims of the larger stakeholder environment and its members. Business and society models are bigger and more inclusive, more reflective of the real world of corporate-stakeholder relationships. Business and society scholars can see corporate performance existing as a multidimensional construct, and we can move toward true multidimensional measures.

As an example of how business and society scholars haven't been thinking correctly about performance measures, consider the recent study by Wood and Jones (1995) that examines sixty-five studies about the relationships between corporate social performance (CSP) and corporate financial performance (CFP). Before the current popularity of the Kinder, Lydenberg and Domini (KLD) database of corporate social responsibility, most studies of CSP/CFP relationships chose some approximate indicator of some aspect of social performance, and correlated that indicator with some measure(s) of financial performance. No theory informed most of these efforts; they were driven primarily by a finance-like desire to show a positive relationship or to deny the existence of one. Wood and Jones write,

> There is no theory to explain why stockholders would or would not prefer a company that gives one percent of pretax earnings to charity, or that hires and develops minority or women workers, or that ranks higher in pollution control indices. Yet most CSP research assumes that such preferences will exist, and that stockholders are the most (or only) appropriate stakeholder group for assessing the results of CSP, regardless of how it has been measured (Wood and Jones, 1995: 242).

Jeanne M. Logsdon and Donna J. Wood

Wood and Jones categorize the sixty-five separate studies in their sample according to the stakeholder group most closely related to the CSP measures in each study. For example, studies involving employees used independent variables such as percent minority managers, percent women managers, existence of a mandatory retirement policy, listing in *Fortune* magazine's *"100 Best Companies to Work For,"* existence and longevity of an Employee Assistance Program, paragraphs of text on employees in the annual report, and whether the firm has an employee newsletter. Similarly, studies involving the community as a stakeholder used variables such as sponsorship of community activities, voluntarism, and charitable giving.

Examining stakeholder-related studies in groups, Wood and Jones found no consistent relationships, *except* for consumer-related measures. Why would this be? Well, there's a strong theory about why shareholders would respond to news of consumer satisfaction or dissatisfaction. Furthermore, there is theory to suggest that shareholders would respond negatively to any corporate decision that creates a downstream liability that would threaten profitability. Likewise, studies showing a negative impact on stock price from some costly event such as a product recall, a large environmental fine, or a plane crash, all make sense because the connection between the event and profitability is well-established, via consumer dissatisfaction, the creation of liabilities, or both.

Wood and Jones propose that future studies relating CSP and CFP need to carefully match the independent and dependent variables according to a theory of stakeholder interests and impacts. They argue that for any particular corporate action, multiple stakeholders may be involved in a variety of ways, each of which may independently affect a firm's financial performance, and some of which may have little or nothing to do with financial performance but may affect the firm in other important ways. They explain:

> Based upon their particular interests and levels of involvement in a company, stakeholders may:
>
> 1. *Establish expectations* (which may be explicit or implicit, and which may or may not be communicated) about corporate performance,
> 2. *Experience the effects* of corporate behaviors (with or without awareness of their source),
> 3. *Evaluate the effects* or potential effects of corporate behaviors on their interests, or the fit of corporate behaviors with their expectations, and
> 4. *Act* upon their interests, expectations, experiences, and/or evaluations.
>
> ... In short, stakeholders define the norms for corporate behavior; they are acted upon by firms; and they make judgments about these

experiences (Wood and Jones, 1995: 243).

Future work on the CSP/CFP relationship has to take into account the existence and dynamics of a network of stakeholders, several of whom may have different interests in any particular corporate behavior. Even if solid bivariate relationships were to be established between valid and reliable measures of CSP and CFP, we would still not know very much about relationships among the firm and the members of its stakeholder environment. Business and society scholars need to develop multivariate measures along with multi-faceted models of firm-stakeholder relations.

Fortunately, we don't have to invent everything from scratch in order to move toward a multidimensional, stakeholder-relevant measure of CSP. Companies already know, for example, about Total Quality Management, the Balanced Scorecard, environmental reporting, customer satisfaction surveys, shareholder wealth measures, employee productivity scores, and a host of performance metrics originating in operations research–these don't have to be reinvented. But they can be turned to good use in stakeholder-based CSP measurement.

For example, Frooman (1997), found in a meta-analysis of event studies from the finance literature, which used CSP-related events, that irresponsible acts consistently resulted in a permanent decline in stock price. Following his example, by applying a stakeholder approach to CSP measurement, we can make good use of existing research and measures and can turn our attention to more creative ways to design multidimensional measurement. As another example, Logsdon and Lewellyn, in their current study (reported in this volume) of several companies' evaluation processes, are exploring how the Balanced Scorecard can be adapted by expanding the range of stakeholders that are included.

Most social auditing studies examine the internal assessment of CSP with regard to stakeholders, but we also need to know how stakeholders themselves assess a firm's social performance. As Philip L. Cochran of Pennsylvania State University has often said, financial measurement is not as cut-and-dried as is sometimes asserted. There is a lot of controversy in accounting and finance about how to create firm value and measure performance. This leaves room to develop theories–and concomitant measures–of how stakeholder valuations affect various aspects of a firm's performance.

Another piece of the puzzle is in the research assessing CSP because of its *intrinsic* value, not because of any hypothesized or hoped-for instrumental links to financial performance. Many of these independent CSP measures are used to correlate with financial performance, but they also stand on their own as dependent or independent variables addressing aspects of CSP. One example is the KLD Socrates database, which is clearly multidimensional, though perhaps not as reliable as researchers might wish. This database

Jeanne M. Logsdon and Donna J. Wood

uses eleven criteria, including positive and negative social screens, to evaluate the social performance of some 600 American-owned corporations. Another example is the annual survey of most admired companies in *Fortune*, from which the score on Community and Environmental Responsibility can be cleansed of the influence of financial performance with the halo-adjustment technique (Brown and Perry, 1995), leaving a purer measure of each firms' community performance, although there appears to be no relationship with firms' environmental performance as measured independently (Brown and Logsdon, 1997).

It is also important to consider industry-specific versus cross-industry population samples in research. There are many problems with cross-industry assessment techniques because industry differences often contaminate or mask company-to-company comparisons. But with an industry-specific focus, one eliminates variation caused solely by industry differences and can then focus on the variables of real interest (Pasquero, 1988). Griffin and Mahon (1997) used this approach in their study of CSP/CFP relationships in the chemical industry, using large databases, such as the KLD Index, the *Fortune* survey of most admired companies, and the Toxics Release Inventory. Griffin and Mahon compared the relative positioning of seven large chemical companies in these databases and found a high degree of consistency across these social performance measures.

Now we have to go back and bring stakeholders into the picture again. Wouldn't it be clever to develop ways of tapping how stakeholders themselves set expectations, evaluate outcomes, and experience the effects of corporate behavior? A step in this direction is Rowley's (1997) study of corporate-stakeholder networks and the various consequences of firm positions within those networks. Another step is Davenport's (1998) research on corporate social performance evaluation, in which she identified a national panel of experts representing five key stakeholder groups. Using a Delphi methodology, she elicited consensus expectations from each group with respect to corporate behavior. Then she matched the resulting expectations to existing social audit and evaluation measures. Her next step is to experiment with several new measures in order to develop a social auditing protocol which will be field-tested in companies. This approach is cumbersome and difficult, but it takes us a long way toward finding out how to evaluate corporate social performance in good faith by bringing stakeholders firmly into the equation.

Finally, there is one additional category of study that could be done. This is the brainstorm of Steven L. Wartick, University of Northern Iowa. He envisions a complex shadowing of the *Fortune* reputation survey every year. While *Fortune* is surveying financial and business experts, researchers in business and society would be surveying relevant stakeholders about the performance of these same firms (Logsdon and Wartick, 1995). Included among the latter group would be environmental activists, community members, managers of nonprofit social service organizations, local government officials, employee and union representatives, and consumer representatives. Such a study would help us to assess the generalizability of *Fortune's* ratings, and it would give us powerful data with which to investigate not only how managers perceive and make trade-offs among and between stakeholders, but also how stakeholders themselves negotiate their various interests in a firm.

There is still so much to do, but we have come a long way. We are now aware that, where moral claims are involved, there is really no difference between "direct" and "indirect" costs of production. The harms and benefits of business activity always fall somewhere, and their distribution always raises moral questions of rights and justice. The idea of "negative externalities" is shown in stakeholder theory to be a fiction. Companies *are* being held accountable for their actions and the effects of those actions on the distribution of harms and benefits within the stakeholder network. For corporations, there is no free lunch.

Focusing on corporate *performance*–not only on intentions, or motivations, or organizational structures and processes–keeps our attention firmly centered on how those harms and benefits are distributed through a company's stakeholder environment. Continuing to ask these questions–who benefits, who is harmed, how, and why–will lead us toward redefining the modern corporation as an integral, valued, and responsible member of that complex stakeholder network we call "society."

Jeanne M. Logsdon *(jlogsdon@unm.edu)* is a professor in the Organizational Studies Department at the Robert O. Anderson Schools of Management, University of New Mexico, Albuquerque, NM 87131-1221.

Donna J. Wood *(djwood@katz.pitt.edu)* is a professor of business administration at the Joseph M. Katz Graduate School of Business, University of Pittsburgh, Pittsburgh, PA 15260.

[1] Based upon a presentation delivered to the Social Issues in Management Division, Academy of Management Annual Meeting, 8-13 August 1997, Boston, MA.

References

Atkinson, A.A., Waterhouse, J.H., and Wells, R.B. 1997. A stakeholder approach to strategic performance measurement. *Sloan Management Review*, 38 (3): 25-37.

Brown, B. and Perry, S. 1995. Halo-removed residuals of *Fortune's* "responsibility to the community and environment"–A decade of data. *Business & Society*, 34 (2): 199-215.

Brown, B. and Logsdon, J.M. 1997. Factors influencing *Fortune's* corporate reputation for community and environmental responsibility. In *Proceedings of the Eighth Annual Meeting of the International Association for Business and Society held in Destin, FL, 6-9 March 1997*, ed. J. Weber and K. Rehbein: 184-189.

Davenport, K.S. 1998. *Corporate citizenship: A stakeholder approach for defining corporate social performance and identifying measures for assessing it*. Doctoral dissertation, The Fielding Institute, Santa Barbara, CA. Proquest, UMI, AAT 9839178.

Frooman, J.S. 1997. Socially irresponsible and illegal behavior and shareholder wealth: A meta-analysis of event studies. *Business & Society*, 36 (3): 221-249.

Griffin, J.J., and Mahon, J.F. 1997. The corporate social performance and corporate financial performance debate: Twenty-five years of incomparable research. *Business & Society*, 36 (1): 5-31.

Logsdon, J.M., and Wartick, S.L. 1995. Theoretically based applications and implications for using the Brown and Perry database. *Business & Society*, 34 (2): 222-226.

Pasquero, J. 1988. Comparative research: The case for middle-range methodologies. *Research in Corporate Social Performance and Policy*, 10: 181-210.

Rowley, T.J. 1997. Moving beyond dyadic ties: A network theory of stakeholder influences. *Academy of Management Review*, 22 (4) (Oct.): 887-910.

Wood, D.J., and Jones, R.E. 1995. Stakeholder mismatching: A theoretical problem in empirical research on corporate social performance. *International Journal of Organizational Analysis*, 3 (3): 229-26